Young

by Iain Gray

D1439737

Lang**Syne**

PUBLISHING

WRITING *to* REMEMBER

Lang**Syne**

PUBLISHING

WRITING *to* REMEMBER

79 Main Street, Newtongrange,
Midlothian EH22 4NA
Tel: 0131 344 0414   Fax: 0845 075 6085
E-mail: info@lang-syne.co.uk
www.langsyneshop.co.uk

Design by Dorothy Meikle
Printed by Printwell Ltd
© Lang Syne Publishers Ltd 2017

ISBN 978-1-85217-204-6

Young

MOTTO:
Prudence excels strength.

CREST:
A Lion Rampant holding a sword.

*Echoes of a far distant past
can still be found in most names*

Chapter one:

Origins of
Scottish surnames

by George Forbes

It all began with the Normans.

For it was they who introduced surnames into common usage more than a thousand years ago, initially based on the title of their estates, local villages and chateaux in France to distinguish and identify these landholdings, usually acquired at the point of a bloodstained sword.

Such grand descriptions also helped enhance the prestige of these arrogant warlords and generally glorify their lofty positions high above the humble serfs slaving away below in the pecking order who only had single names, often with Biblical connotations as in Pierre and Jacques.

The only descriptive distinctions among this peasantry concerned their occupations, like Pierre the swineherd or Jacques the ferryman.

The Normans themselves were originally Vikings (or Northmen) who raided, colonised and eventually settled down around the French coastline.

They had sailed up the Seine in their longboats in 900AD under their ferocious leader Rollo and ruled the roost in north east France before sailing over to conquer England, bringing their relatively new tradition of having surnames with them.

It took another hundred years for the Normans to percolate northwards and surnames did not begin to appear in Scotland until the thirteenth century.

These adventurous knights brought an aura of chivalry with them and it was said no damsel of any distinction would marry a man unless he had at least two names.

The family names included that of Scotland's great hero Robert De Brus and his compatriots were warriors from families like the De Morevils, De Umphravils, De Berkelais, De Quincis, De Viponts and De Vaux.

As the knights settled the boundaries of their vast estates, they took territorial names, as in Hamilton, Moray, Crawford, Cunningham, Dunbar, Ross, Wemyss, Dundas, Galloway, Renfrew, Greenhill, Hazelwood, Sandylands and Church-hill.

Other names, though not with any obvious geographical or topographical features, nevertheless derived from ancient parishes like Douglas, Forbes, Dalyell and Guthrie.

Other surnames were coined in connection with occupations, castles or legendary deeds.

Stuart originated in the word steward, a prestigious post which was an integral part of any large medieval household. The same applied to Cooks, Chamberlains, Constables and Porters.

Borders towns and forts – needed in areas like the Debateable Lands which were constantly fought over by feuding local families – had their own distinctive names; and it was often from them that the resident groups took their communal titles, as in the Grahams of Annandale, the Elliots and Armstrongs of the East Marches, the Scotts and Kerrs of Teviotdale and Eskdale.

Even physical attributes crept into surnames, as in Small, Little and More (the latter being 'beg' in Gaelic), Long or Lang, Stark, Stout, Strong or Strang and even Jolly.

Mieklejohns would have had the strength of several men, while Littlejohn was named after the legendary sidekick of Robin Hood.

Colours got into the act with Black, White, Grey, Brown and Green (Red developed into Reid, Ruddy or Ruddiman). Blue was rare and nobody ever wanted to be associated with yellow.

Pompous worthies took the name Wiseman, Goodman and Goodall.

Words intimating the sons of leading figures were soon affiliated into the language as in Johnson, Adamson, Richardson and Thomson, while the Norman equivalent of Fitz (from the French-Latin 'filius' meaning 'son') cropped up in Fitzmaurice and Fitzgerald.

The prefix 'Mac' was 'son of' in Gaelic and clans often originated with occupations – as in

MacNab being sons of the Abbot, MacPherson and MacVicar being sons of the minister and MacIntosh being sons of the chief.

The church's influence could be found in the names Kirk, Clerk, Clarke, Bishop, Friar and Monk. Proctor came from a church official, Singer and Sangster from choristers, Gilchrist and Gillies from Christ's servant, Mitchell, Gilmory and Gilmour from servants of St Michael and Mary, Malcolm from a servant of Columba and Gillespie from a bishop's servant.

The rudimentary medical profession was represented by Barber (a trade which also once included dentistry and surgery) as well as Leech or Leitch.

Businessmen produced Merchants, Mercers, Monypennies, Chapmans, Sellers and Scales, while down at the old village watermill the names that cropped up included Miller, Walker and Fuller.

Other self explanatory trades included Coopers, Brands, Barkers, Tanners, Skinners, Brewsters and Brewers, Tailors, Saddlers, Wrights,

Cartwrights, Smiths, Harpers, Joiners, Sawyers, Masons and Plumbers.

Even the scenery was utilised as in Craig, Moor, Hill, Glen, Wood and Forrest.

Rank, whether high or low, took its place with Laird, Barron, Knight, Tennant, Farmer, Husband, Granger, Grieve, Shepherd, Shearer and Fletcher.

The hunt and the chase supplied Hunter, Falconer, Fowler, Fox, Forrester, Archer and Spearman.

The renowned medieval historian Froissart, who eulogised about the romantic deeds of chivalry (and who condemned Scotland as being a poverty stricken wasteland), once sniffily dismissed the peasantry of his native France as the jacquerie (or the jacques-without-names) but it was these same humble folk who ended up overthrowing the arrogant aristocracy.

In the olden days, only the blueblooded knights of antiquity were entitled to full, proper names, both Christian and surnames, but with the passing of time and a more egalitarian, less feudal atmosphere, more respectful and worthy titles spread throughout the populace as a whole.

Echoes of a far distant past can still be found in most names and they can be borne with pride in commemoration of past generations who fought and toiled in some capacity or other to make our nation what it now is, for good or ill.

Chapter two:

The battling Borderers

**The high drama and romance that infuses
the history of the Youngs in Scotland over
the centuries has been played out against
two quite separate backdrops.**

The rolling landscape of the Borders
was home to a family of Youngs who gained an
infamous reputation as wild and lawless
reivers, or raiders, while the far northeast bred
generations of distinguished royal courtiers
and scholars.

Originally a form of nickname to
differentiate a son who had the same forename,
or Christian name, as his father – as in 'Young'
John, or 'Young' William – it gradually assumed
the form of a surname as hereditary surnames
became more popular both in England and
Scotland.

A popular variation of the surname for
centuries was 'Yonge', and one of the earliest

appearances of this form in Scottish records occurs in 1271, when two Yonges are recorded in Dumbarton, in the west of the country; further north, a John Young of Dingwall is recorded as having witnessed a charter by the Earl of Ross to Reginald, Lord of the Isles, in 1342.

One of the earliest surviving records of Youngs, or Yonges, in the Borders dates from 1335 when a Roger Young, described simply as 'a Scottish gentleman', was released from English confinement in what was then the important trading town of Berwick.

The hapless merchant may have fallen foul of rival English traders and doubtless would have had to pay a hefty sum to secure his release.

While Roger Young may have earned an honest living as a respectable merchant, the same cannot be said for the vast majority of Border Youngs, who maintained a precarious existence by raiding, or reiving, livestock from their neighbours on the other side of the border.

Youngs who passed into local legend

on account of their daring reveing forays included the colourfully named Blackhall Jock, Hobb of the Bog, Hob the Gun, and Tom the Gun.

The border between Scotland and England had been established under the Treaty of York in 1237 as a line running from the Solway to the Tweed. But this proved no effective barrier for the lawless families who lived on either side of the line.

Three Marches, or areas of administration, known as the West, East, and Middle Marches were established on either side of the border, and all were governed by a warden who was appointed by the respective royal authorities.

During the rare times of peace between the kingdoms of Scotland and England, complaints from either side of the border were dealt with on Truce Days, the wardens of the respective marches acing as arbitrators.

There was also a curious law known as the Hot Trod, that allowed anyone who had their precious livestock stolen the right to pursue the thieves across the border to retrieve their property by force.

In Scotland, the East March was dominated by the Homes and Swintons, while the Armstrongs, Maxwells, Johnstones, and Grahams ruled the West March.

The proud Kerrs, Douglases, and Elliots held sway in the Middle March, and it was to the powerful clan of Douglas that the smaller family of Youngs allied their fortunes.

Settled mainly in the Bowmont Valley, east of Jedburgh, the Youngs are estimated to have been able to muster up to 400 skilled riders, and this force, combined with the strengths of other smaller families, made the Douglases a formidable force to be reckoned with.

The ties between the Border Youngs and Clan Douglas became so close that they are recognised as a sept family affiliated to this famous clan whose motto is 'Never behind', and whose crest is a salamander atop a flaming cap.

The Douglas name stems from the lands of Douglas, in Lanarkshire, and it was William the Hardy, 1st Lord Douglas, who died in 1298, who founded the two famed Douglas branches of the Red Douglases and the Black Douglases.

The Red Douglases became established in Angus, in the northeast of Scotland, while the Black Douglases ruled a mighty fiefdom that took in vast estates in Annandale, Galloway, Ettrick, Eskdale, Teviotdale, and Lauderdale, and it was to this branch that the Border Youngs belonged.

Through their affiliation to the Douglases, the Youngs became staunch defenders of Scotland's freedom during the bitter Wars of Independence, and one of Robert the Bruce's greatest military commanders was Sir James Douglas.

Sir James not only fought at the side of the great warrior king at the battle of Bannockburn in 1314, but also was killed in his attempt to carry his beloved monarch's heart to the Holy Land in 1330.

Nearly sixty years later, in 1388, Youngs fought with distinction at the battle of

Otterburn, under the command of James, 2nd Earl of Douglas.

A Scottish force had earlier been involved in a skirmish outside the walls of Newcastle, inside English territory, when the earl managed to snatch the silk pennant from the lance of his adversary Henry Percy, heir to the 1st Earl of Northumberland and better known to posterity as Henry Hotspur.

Douglas proceeded to lead his army back towards Scotland, but Hotspur, stung by the insult to his honour, vowed that his precious pennant would never be allowed to cross the border.

He pursued Douglas, and the two armies clashed at Otterburn, the young Earl of Douglas receiving a fatal blow.

On Douglas's dying command, and wishing to keep his fate a secret from his loyal followers, he ordered Sir James Lindsay of Crawford to raise the famed Banner of the Bloody Heart of the Douglases.

Crawford carried out the command, rallied the Scots, and led them to victory.

When not finding an outlet for their martial passions in fighting in the cause of Scotland's freedom, the Border families found release in their time-honoured custom of lawlessness.

In more settled times, this became such a threat to not only the peace of the Scottish kingdom itself but the uneasy peace with England, that a series of harsh measures were imposed by the royal authority to curb what had become a virtual state of anarchy.

This state of affairs is reflected in a report submitted to James VI in 1608, which lamented that 'wild incests, adulteries, convocation of the lieges, shooting and wearing of hackbutts, pistols, and lances, daily bloodsheds, oppression, and disobedience in civil matters, neither are nor has been punished.'

Chapter three:

By royal command

Rather more law-abiding than their far southern namesakes, those Youngs who had established themselves in the northeast became trusted royal officials and defenders of the laws of the land.

It was through attempts to defend the rich pasturelands of the shire of Angus from the ravages of Duncan Stewart, a son of Alexander Buchan, better known as the Wolf of Badenoch, that William Young, of Ochterlony, near Forfar, was killed in a fierce battle at Glen Brierachan in 1391.

Sir Walter Ogilvie of Auchterhouse, Sheriff of Angus, had hastily assembled a force of local magnates and lairds such as William Young as a marauding force of clansmen under Duncan Stewart descended on the shire intent on pillage.

Sir Walter's poorly trained citizens' army

was no match for the battle-hardened raiders, however, who slaughtered them before proceeding to loot, plunder, and burn.

As the centuries progressed, the Youngs of the northeast rose in prominence to the extent that they held lands near Durris, Kelly, and Auldbar, near the town of Forfar, and it was a Young of Auldbar who achieved distinction as a royal tutor and ambassador.

Born the son of a Dundee merchant in 1544, Peter Young was appointed tutor to the four-year-old James VI in 1570, along with the classical scholar and staunch Presbyterian George Buchanan.

Buchanan was an able tutor, but a hard taskmaster, apparently taking great delight in telling his young charge that his ill-starred mother, Mary, Queen of Scots, had been 'a murderous whore'!

His strict discipline paid dividends, however, because at an early age the precocious James proved himself no academic slouch by having mastered a variety of subjects ranging from Greek, Latin, French, and history, to cosmography, geography, composition, arithmetic, rhetoric and theology.

In later years he would exercise his academic prowess by penning treatises on both kingship and demonology.

Peter Young had been placed in charge of assembling the 600 or so weighty tomes required for the young king's education, and is also recognised as having fired his imagination beyond the bounds of the mere written word.

Becoming an impartial and trusted counsellor to James, in comparison to the vast majority of lackeys and 'yes-men' who thronged the royal court, Young was used as ambassador to numerous other courts, including that of Denmark to arrange the king's marriage to the Princess Anne.

It is probably an episode that, in later years, the loyal ambassador was only too happy to forget.

The king's decision to marry had not been taken lightly, reached only after he had spent fifteen days locked away in prayer to seek God's guidance.

It is highly unlikely that his eventual impatience to marry the 15-year-old Danish princess was based on a genuine love for the girl. He hadn't even met her in the flesh. The most likely incentive was the £15,000 dowry that came with her hand.

The monarch had earlier sent Peter Young and another courtier to Denmark to negotiate the royal match, and in June of 1589 wrote to them of his desire for the match to go ahead.

A small fleet bearing royal courtiers and lavish gifts set sail for Denmark later in the summer to arrange the marriage by proxy and bring the bride back to Scotland.

This proxy marriage, with Peter Young in attendance, took place in Copenhagen in August, and Anne finally set sail for Scotland in early September. Much to everyone's frustration, the fleet was hit by heavy storms and had to seek the shelter of a Norwegian fjord.

James himself embarked for Norway in

late October, and the couple were at last married in Oslo on November 23. Peter Young and his weary fellow courtiers then had to make the long trek along with the happy couple for another marriage ceremony at the Danish royal castle of Kronenberg.

The king then went on to enjoy a lengthy Scandinavian honeymoon, not arriving back in his native kingdom until May of the following year.

Peter Young was well rewarded for his exhausting efforts on his monarch's behalf, receiving the accolade of knighthood in 1604, one year after the Union of the Crowns, while he was also a tutor for a time to the future Charles I.

Although the Youngs had held lands at Auldbar for generations, it was not until 1670 that a grandson of Sir Peter Young bought the actual barony of Auldbar.

A Robert Young of Auldbar was an important patron of the renowned Latin scholar Thomas Ruddiman, who was born in the parish of Boyndie, Banff, in 1674.

Ruddiman had been appointed tutor to

Young's son in 1694, and it was through Young senior's influence that he later obtained his first post as a schoolmaster, at Laurencekirk, in Kincardineshire.

The Aulbar estate was sold in 1753, and the Youngs of Auldbar became a dormant clan.

In 1989, however, the Lord Lyon King of Arms of Scotland, following a petition from a Clan Young that had been convened at Orlando, Florida, a year earlier, confirmed the right for clan members to use the Youngs of Auldbar crest of a lion rampant holding a sword, and the motto of 'Prudence excels strength.'

Sir Peter Young had died in 1628 and his eldest son and successor, Sir James Young, was granted lands in Ireland. It is perhaps because of this that the name Young is common in Ireland, particularly in the counties of Londonderry, Antrim, Down, and Tyrone.

Youngs have gained distinction on the battlefields of recent times, and no less so than Brigadier Peter Young, who was born in 1915 and died in 1988.

Described as one of the most colourful, creative, and influential soldiers of his generation, he served with elite commando units in both Europe and Burma during the Second World War.

The recipient of the Military Cross on no less than three occasions, he became head of the military history department at Britain's prestigious Sandhurst military academy, and was a prolific military historian.

He formed the Sealed Knot in 1968, a society of enthusiasts dedicated to the study of the Civil War and re-enacting some of its famous battles.

Chapter four:

Scientists and code breakers

Far from the battlefield, other Youngs have made a profound impact on the worlds of science, religion, and music.

Born in 1811 as the son of a humble Glasgow carpenter, James Young achieved fame as a skilled chemical engineer, and is perhaps better known as 'Paraffin' Young.

After attending classes in chemistry at Glasgow's Anderson's College (now Strathclyde University), Young received the important post of assistant to Professor Thomas Graham, the Glasgow-born chemist who founded the law on the diffusion of gases that now bears his name.

Entering industry after accompanying Graham to University College, London, in 1837, Young became fascinated with the properties of shale and bituminous coal and, after a number of intricate experiments, found that by using a slow distillation process he could produce paraffin wax and paraffin oil – essential for lighting, heating, and a range of industrial processes.

In 1862, twelve years after taking out a patent on his process, distillation plants located at the vast shale deposits in Mid and West Lothian in Scotland went into production, making Young the creator of the world's first oil industry based on oil and shale deposits.

A Fellow of the Royal Society of Edinburgh and a Fellow of the Royal Society, Young, who died in 1883, was also president of Anderson's College from 1868 to 1877, and founded the college's Young Chair of Technical Chemistry.

Born at Milverton, Somerset, in 1773, Thomas Young was not only one of the greatest physicists and physicians of his age, but a gifted Egyptologist who laid the foundations of modern-day Egyptology by breaking the mysterious code of the famous Rosetta Stone.

A black basalt slab uncovered by soldiers from Napoleon's army at Rosetta (Rashid) in

Egypt in 1799, and dated to nearly two hundred years before the birth of Christ, the stone proved to hold the key to deciphering the mysterious Egyptian hieroglyphics.

This was possible because readily understandable Greek and a cursive script, known as Demotic that had been developed in later Egyptian history, accompanied hieroglyphic text on the stone.

Displaying the same text in three forms but only in the two languages of Demotic and Greek, Young broke the 'code' of the hieroglyphics when he had the startling insight that they 'wrote' the sounds of the royal name of Ptolemy.

Using this revelation as his basis, the French scholar Jean-Francois Champollion found the hieroglyphics recorded the sound of the Egyptian language.

In addition to his pioneering work on the Rosetta Stone, the multi-talented Young, before his death in 1829, also established the wave theory of light, put forward a theory of colour vision, and was the first to describe the condition known as astigmatism of the eye.

His epitaph in Westminster Abbey rather aptly describes him as 'a man alike eminent in almost every department of human learning.'

A continent away, Brigham Young, who was born in Vermont in 1801, and who died in 1877, was baptised into the Mormon Church in 1832 after reading the Book of Mormon, written by its founder Joseph Smith.

Following Smith's murder by a bigoted anti-Mormon mob in 1844, Brigham Young took over the leadership of the movement and led its followers on their famed and arduous trek to Utah's Salt Lake Valley, where Salt Lake City was later established as the spiritual home of a religion that now has thousands of adherents worldwide.

In the world of contemporary music, Neil Young, who was born in Toronto, Canada, in 1945, has achieved international fame as a talented and prolific rock and folk musician.

In addition to a career as a solo artiste, he has enjoyed acclaim as a member of The Buffalo Springfield and Crosby, Stills, Nash and Young.

"I have absolutely loved Light's daily doses of inspiration and still look forward to reading them everyday."

Sarah Cooper, comedian

"I read just one of the doses, and couldn't put it down. Truly inspirational!"

Leon Logothetis, host of *The Kindness Diaries*

"Let these pocket-sized pearls of wisdom, warmth, and wonder propel you to places of peace and possibility."

Ava DuVernay, award-winning filmmaker

"I really enjoy Light's daily inspiration."

Rosario Dawson, actress

"Light's inspirational, timely stories are profoundly relevant for us all."

Elena Brower, bestselling author of *Practice You, Art of Attention,* and *Being You*

"In this book, Light offers infinite opportunity to drop in for meaningful reflection and contemplation . . . in a time when we need it most."

Adriene Mishler, founder of Yoga With Adriene

"With everything happening in the world today, these doses of inspiration are much needed."

Lewis Howes, host of the *School of Greatness* podcast

Also by Light Watkins

The Inner Gym

Bliss More

knowing where to look

108 Daily
Doses of
Inspiration

LIGHT WATKINS

sounds true
BOULDER, COLORADO

Sounds True

Boulder, CO 80306

Published 2021

Cover & Book design by Team Knowing
(Light Watkins, Yuliia Andriichuk, Lisa Kerans)

Illustrations by Yuliia Andriichuk

Printed in Canada

Names: Watkins, Light, author.
Title: Knowing where to look : 108 daily doses of inspiration / Light
    Watkins.
Description: Boulder, CO : Sounds True, 2021. | Summary: "In Knowing Where
    to Look, Watkins presents a trove of compelling inspirational material
    to catalyze positive change and give you fuel to push through
    self-limiting beliefs"-- Provided by publisher.
Identifiers: LCCN 2020055505 (print) | LCCN 2020055506 (ebook) | ISBN
    9781683647706 (hardback) | ISBN 9781683647713 (ebook)
Subjects: LCSH: Inspiration. | Self-realization.
Classification: LCC BF410 .W38 2021 (print) | LCC BF410 (ebook) | DDC

    153.3--dc23

LC record available at https://lccn.loc.gov/2020055505

LC ebook record available at https://lccn.loc.gov/2020055506

10 9 8 7 6 5 4 3 2 1

To my
brother from
another mother,
Will Dalton.

You were there for many
of these stories—and now
you're omnipresent.

I am eternally grateful for
your lasting influence
in my life.

A Good Reason

Right Place, Right Time

In May 2018, as I was turning forty-five, I downsized. A lot. Meaning, I got rid of pretty much all of my possessions that didn't fit into a carry-on bag and a backpack.

In the months before, I'd seen a documentary on minimalism and read a book about the joys of giving things away that I no longer used, and I had been closely observing a good friend who had recently gone nomadic. In short, I was inspired.

I was inspired to shed all of my life's possessions. It would be a hard reset—an epic purging of the items I had been lugging around from apartment to apartment for years, even decades.

I would give away my entire wardrobe (except for a few days' worth of clothes), all of my furniture, the artwork I'd collected over years of traveling and teaching around the world, the overflowing box of handwritten letters I'd been storing in my various closets for over twenty years, my journals full of travel stories, secrets, and poetry, my analog photos from my earlier days as a wandering street photographer—basically, anything I wasn't using on a day-to-day basis. And everything else had to fit into my twenty-two-inch carry-on bag.

That's all I allowed myself to keep. My carry-on would effectively become my new apartment. There would be no storage rooms. Sentimental or not, everything else had to go.

I gave my thirty-day notice and had multiple yard sales during that final month in my apartment.

The only thing remaining in the shell of my empty living room was the echo, which signaled the ominous end of an era—and not just of my apartment, but of the conventional idea of stability, of comfort, of familiarity.

From that point on, I would live exclusively from inspiration. And I would find comfort in the discomfort of the unknown. I'm sure that can sound scary, or crazy to some. But had I not trusted my internal GPS, I don't think I could've done it. However, I'd spent years practicing these kinds of leaps, and while I didn't know the outcome (and still don't), something inside said, "It's time to switch it up," and that was enough of a justification for me. In fact, this would be my third nomadic adventure within the span of twenty-five years.

That's right, my third. I actually did something similar when I was a twenty-two-year-old advertising creative living in Chicago, fresh out of college. It was one of the first times I consciously followed inspiration.

I was young and curious about the various colors of life, and my first "real" job after school was at a boutique ad agency on the Miracle Mile (also known as Michigan Avenue) in downtown Chicago, not far from the Chicago Art Institute.

I didn't know it at the time, but it would be the only nine-to-five job I would ever have, and it would only last about three months, at which point I would be inspired to resign and use my meager savings to purchase a one-way ticket to Paris.

Why Paris? Because I had developed this strange inner calling to travel there.

Even though I was a kid from Alabama, there was something familiar and almost dreamy about the idea of exploring the home of the Champs-Élysées and Eiffel Tower.

I didn't speak French or know much about French culture outside of what I had seen on television. I was going on nothing more than a hunch, and that was enough to begin loosely planning a trip.

My internal GPS was my travel agent, and it instructed me to resign from the ad agency and begin making travel arrangements. Mind you, I had no place to stay, and there were no smart phones, search engines, or map applications to pre-plan and make the trip more predictable or comforting. Everything in those days was analog.

I lied and told my mom that I had landed a job there, and that they were sending for me. I felt bad for lying, but I knew she would worry about me if she discovered the truth—that not a soul was expecting me in Paris, that I only had a few hundred dollars to my name, that I didn't know where I would stay on my first night, that I was stepping so far out of my comfort zone that I was feeling both alive and numb at the same time.

But the part that I was really afraid she wouldn't understand was how, deep down, I knew it would all somehow work out. Because I didn't even understand how I knew. I just did.

On the night of my one-way flight, I nervously arrived to an overcrowded gate carrying a black army duffle bag stuffed with T-shirts, a couple pairs of jeans, a navy peacoat, a black military sweater with buttons across the right shoulder, and some black combat boots.

I made a stop at the army surplus store a few weeks before, because I figured military gear was more durable than traditional department store clothing, and I didn't know the next time I would have a chance to shop. I also had my passport and a *Paris on a Budget* guidebook.

My Continental Airlines flight from Chicago to Paris had a connection through Newark Liberty International Airport.

It was late in the evening when I sat at the gate with my duffel bag full of all of my life's possessions, bobbing in a sea of French natives conversing in my new language, most of which I didn't understand aside from bonjour (hello) and ça va (how are you?). It was the first time I felt physically anxious since I had decided to take this insane leap of faith by purchasing a one-way ticket to Paris's Charles De Gaulle Airport.

Just before boarding commenced in Newark, the gate agent announced that the flight was oversold and a few passengers would need to give up their seats.

No one budged. The agent came back on a few minutes later and offered a voucher of $200 to entice volunteers to give up their seats. Still, no one batted an eye.

A couple minutes later, they sweetened the deal to $400 per voucher. I leaped up and made a beeline for the gate agent to volunteer my seat.

She handed me a flight voucher, plus a meal ticket good for dinner and lunch the next day, plus room and board at one of the local airport hotels for the night.

I had just earned enough money for my return ticket, I happily thought.

When I arrived the next evening for the flight to Paris, it was the same song, second verse—a crowded gate, over-sold flight, and a call for volunteers to give up their seats. I was able to score another $400 voucher! "Wow," I thought, "maybe I can just do this for a living?"

Everything felt so easy, so seamless. During my second overnight stay at the same airport hotel, I met two Americans living in Paris who had also given up their seats. And after dinner, we exchanged contact information. So not only did I have $800 in airline flight vouchers (more than enough for a return flight), but I also had familiar faces to call upon in Paris.

When I eventually landed in France early the following morning, I went straight from the taxi to see about getting a job at one of the big fashion houses.

The first place I cold-called turned me away within about five minutes of my arrival. I wasn't a good fit, they told me. Come back and reapply in a few months.

As I was sitting in the foyer, looking through maps and trying to figure out where to try next, a man in the office approached me and said in perfect American English that he recognized me from Chicago. Bizarre.

Apparently, he was from Chicago but working in Paris, and had seen me in Chicago that previous summer. He was a photographer, he said, and never forgets a face.

He asked if I got hired, and I told him no, I was rejected. Without much thought, he replied, "Follow me," and we walked out of that office, down the hallway, and into the office literally right next door so that he could introduce me to another potential employer.

As I walked through the door and glanced around the office, I heard someone scream my name. I turned around, and standing there was a dear old friend from college, Laurie.

I had no idea that she was even in town, but evidently she'd moved to Paris some months before and was now working in that office.

After learning that I was in need of a place to stay, she connected me with her friend, who just so happened to have an empty apartment in front of the Sacré-Coeur in one of the most desirable areas of Paris. And on top of that, the company agreed to hire me.

Within two hours of landing in Paris, not knowing a soul, I ended up with a job and a place to stay. I went on to live in Paris for about six months, hanging out with an incredible group of new and interesting friends, most of whom I met on my first day there—and all divinely timed with two intentionally missed flights and one unintentional work rejection.

Plus, I had the dough to return whenever I liked, all because I followed my inner guidance—the voice of inspiration.

I learned from that first nomadic experience about the power of inspiration, and that I, like many people, had been guided by inspiration for much of my life without even realizing it. And over the last couple of decades, I've learned how to recognize that inner guidance, to really listen to and trust it, and to know that no matter how things appear on the outside, if I follow it consciously, I'll always find myself in the right place at the right time.

What Is Inspiration?

I'll be the first to admit that inspiration is a tricky concept to define, because defining it using words feels somewhat limiting, kind of like defining the word *love*. However, it's undeniable that we *feel* love, and similarly, most of us have felt inspired at one time or another.

The word *inspire* comes from the Latin root words *in*, which means "into," and *spirare*, which means "to breathe or blow"—so to inspire means to "blow into," as in, to receive air to breathe; but instead of air, it's an idea or a truth that we receive, usually from a divine source (or what some refer to as God or "the Universe").

Whether we agree with this perspective or not, the feeling is undeniable. And while life may tempt us to search in all of the wrong places for inspiration (money, success, and so on), my sense is that wherever there is meaning, you will find inspiration. Wherever there is a will to live, you'll find inspiration. In fact, there can be so much inspiration around us that, most times, we can't even see it.

It's like the classic story of the two young fish who swam past the older, wiser fish, and the wise fish greeted them with the question, "How's the water today, chaps?" And the two young fish responded with an awkward, "fine," and "good." And as they swam off, one of the young fish turned to his fish buddy and asked, "Hey, what's water again?" And his buddy went, "I've heard about it. They say it's everywhere, but I've never seen it."

I'll add that inspiration feels like part inner guidance (like the hunch I felt to go to Paris), part blind faith in a greater possibility, and part inner voice, nudging me to take an action that helps me grow and expand the awareness that I'm a part of something much bigger than just my individual worries and concerns.

Inspiration is a catalyst for positive change that can be felt, heard, and experienced typically through the heart (as opposed to the head). It's a vibe that can't be easily ignored or suppressed, and it urges you to step outside of your comfort zone, often in some inconvenient way, and for reasons that may be beyond your immediate comprehension. But as you follow it, nine times out of ten, you'll end up in a grand adventure—and not the dramatic kind, but the serendipitous kind. You notice that life gets better, and your perception of what's possible becomes broader. Following inspiration often and without question will eventually make your inner voice of inspiration distinct from other internal messages that may not feel so positive or daring. And you'll see that you too have been swimming in an ocean of inspiration this entire time.

Inspiration can also be found in unlikely places: near bushes, rocks, and trees, and even in sitcoms, on airplanes, in church hymns, or in a glass of wine. Inspiration can be sourced while washing dishes, going for a walk, taking a bath, or catching up with friends. When you know what to look for, it's actually harder *not* to see inspiration. Whether we do something with it, though, is another story (and perhaps even another book), but first things first—let's get on the same page with what inspiration is.

A question for you: have you ever had what some people refer to as a deep inner calling? In other words, has something deep within you ever urged you to act or express yourself or take a leap of faith toward a better possibility—one that felt both exciting because you weren't sure how it would turn out *and* a little scary because you weren't sure how it would turn out?

Have you ever felt attracted to a place or a person without knowing why? Have you been called to express yourself with a level of courage and honesty that surprised even you? Have you put pen to paper or brush to canvas and created something that, a few months later, seemed as though someone more talented and wiser than you created it? If so, then you, my friend, have been inspired. It's really that simple.

The dictionary defines *inspiration* as "the process of being mentally stimulated to do or feel something, especially something creative." I would add that although the stimulation could be externally triggered, it's sourced *internally*. In other words, it's not coming from somewhere outside of yourself, or from some future experience, or from something you must first acquire. It's a source that you can access right here and now, and I want to help you tap into it.

The Opposite of Inspiration (The Other Voices)

Sometimes, the best way to define a feeling that's indefinable is to explore what it's *not*. Maybe you're not sure that you've ever felt inspired before, or perhaps it wasn't strong enough of a force to draw you into action? First of all, there's nothing wrong with you or special about those people who seem to always be inspired. Inspiration is indeed within all of us, but we all also have an inner voice of fear, whose job it is to constantly warn us about everything that can go wrong if we listen to inspiration.

Genetically, our brains are predisposed to heed the warnings of the fear voice. The fear voice is extremely risk averse, especially in moments of security and comfort. If we risk disrupting a familiar and comfortable environment full of resources and validation, our brain will cause us to worry incessantly for our safety, and we will feel concerned about moving away from that environment, or potentially running out of resources (like time, money, or love), or worse, being attacked by predators, and either dying or returning embarrassed and ashamed for thinking we could pull it off. And the voice of fear is not shy about expressing those worries to us through an obsessive and often paralyzing inner dialogue wherein we talk ourselves out of taking a leap of faith and become convinced that life will be much safer in the long run if we stay put and play it safe.

Therefore, it's pain, and not the mere dissatisfaction with the status quo, that mostly stimulates the changes we experience. Instead of following our innate curiosity, we've learned to suppress it or dismiss it as unrealistic or foolish, and return to our routines, our status quos, our "normalcy," where life becomes increasingly dull and uninspiring. And only when we get sick, or fired, or broken up with, or we suffer some other unanticipated loss, do we search within ourselves for what we truly want in life. Only then will we be willing to take the leap of faith, because life backed us into a spiritual corner by stripping away what was most precious to us—our sense of familiarity—and we literally have nothing left to lose.

The process of becoming choiceless reminds me of this popular Anaïs Nin quote: "And the day came when the risk to remain tight in a bud was more painful than the risk it took to blossom."

That's usually where the quote ends. But the next part of the passage reveals a more nuanced understanding of trading what Nin refers to as "normal pleasures" (or the familiar) for abnormal ones (the unknown):

Life is a process of becoming, a combination of states we have to go through. Where people fail is that they wish to elect a state and remain in it. This is a kind of death.

Living never wore one out so much as the effort not to live. Life is truly known only to those who suffer, lose, endure adversity and stumble from defeat to defeat.

Perfection is static, and I am in full progress. Abnormal pleasures kill the taste for normal ones.

Under no circumstances shall pain be mistaken for the voice of inspiration. But it's sometimes hard to distinguish between the two because living a "normal" life causes the voice of pain and fear to feel inherently louder and more alarming than inspiration.

Historically, a command like "Run!" has more of a sense of urgency than "Quit your job that you hate, even though it pays well and looks great on your résumé!" The former quickly gets our full attention while the latter is often dismissed as unrealistic. Therefore, we've naturally fed into and nurtured the voices of fear and pain and heeded their advice for a lot longer, and we've behaved with more loyalty than we've shown to our internal voice of inspiration—which is usually only heeded very occasionally, and then quickly dropped when life gets busy or we come to our "senses."

We've been taught to treat fear as more practical and wise, whereas the voice of inspiration often sounds like the *least* practical (and most ridiculous) thing we could possibly follow in the moment. And whichever one has garnered the most of our attention over the years and decades is usually the one that wins.

So fear has enjoyed a *huge* genetic and societal advantage throughout human history. And this is why true innovators and idealists—the people who are bold enough to break out of the fray and do things differently—are so rare in society. While each of us has the potential to live an inspired life, society all but beats it out of us by the time we reach adulthood, and we become extremely gun-shy when it comes to recognizing and following inspiration. It's just much easier to ignore it and continue fitting in.

But then we remember, inspiration is responsible for every single one of society's greatest inventions, discoveries, works of art, and cultural norms. Anything made by any person that you've ever admired (and perhaps many of the things you don't admire or take for granted) began as a spark of inspiration in someone's mind or heart. And what's more, they acted upon it—often in the face of great adversity and resistance to change.

"The ordinary 'horseless carriage' is at present a luxury for the wealthy; and although its price will probably fall in the future, it will never, of course, come into as common use as the bicycle," reported the *Literary Digest* in 1899, referring to the predicted demise of a new invention called an automobile. This is just one of millions of examples throughout history where a gatekeeper of truth, a predictor of the future, announced with absolute certainty that some poor soul's inspired creation was destined to fail. And the same was probably said about the bicycle, and the horse and carriage, and the cart, and even the wheel.

One of the hallmarks of humanity is that we all imagine and dream of better possibilities. Our innate creativity and innovative ability has its roots in inspiration—whether it's a longing for a better way to transport people, or finding a more sustainable way of dealing with climate change, once our wheels start turning, we've been tapped by inspiration. The only question is, what are we going to do about it?

Last, inspiration is extremely contagious. By accessing and following *your* inspiration, you will inspire hundreds or perhaps thousands of others to tap into theirs, and they will inspire thousands more, and so the reach of one person saying yes to their inspiration can indirectly inspire millions. Which means, it's literally impossible to be inspired in isolation. Whatever you must do to find your inspiration, you're not just doing it for yourself. Any inspiration that seems personally beneficial doubles as community service, because you are also doing it for the greater good. And if you keep your focus on that bigger picture, you'll be more inclined to act.

To that end, I sincerely hope you savor this collection of 108 inspirational doses, and that you gain much value from experiencing them. And as I remind my daily email subscribers each morning, inspiration is best when it's shared, so feel free to share the stories that speak to you the most with your friends, family, and community.

How Does This Book Work?

I'm not sure how you found this book, but in your hands is a potential treasure trove of inspiration—the by-product of thousands upon thousands of hours of researching and writing my *Daily Dose of Inspiration* newsletter.

Each day since June 2016 I have emailed my list of subscribers a story, or an anecdote, or an observation that I have found personally inspiring—messages that have given me insight and perspective into what is truly important in life.

My intent is to provide you with a little dose of inspiration whenever needed. In that regard, you could use this book as a helpful resource for setting the tone for your day, or for gaining perspective while grappling with a challenging situation or a trying phase of life. Out of these 108 doses, you will hopefully find a few that apply to what you're going through. And if you're wondering, why 108 doses? It's because in ancient wisdom traditions, that number represents a feeling of wholeness and a deeper connection to source—two by-products of following your inspiration.

This is not like a traditional book that you would read from cover to cover—although no one's going to stop you if that's what you feel like doing. The way it's intended to be experienced is like one of those Magic 8-Balls. You remember those hand-sized plastic black spheres full of that mysterious indigo-colored liquid? When you shook it up, a message would appear in the little window, offering you an answer to whatever yes-or-no question you asked.

This book's premise is the same. Maybe you're going through something in life and you could use a little added perspective. Just flip to any page in this book and see which "dose" catches your eye. Maybe it'll be a title, or the way the text is designed, or an illustration, or a quote. And wherever your attention goes, you'll likely find something useful to take away and apply to your situation. Each dose is written to be timeless and relevant for a variety of situations. Some are like little appetizers of inspiration while others are like a main course, as they come with additional commentary and questions for you to consider. And some will become favorite stories that you read again and again, and get something different from them each time.

And as I tell my email subscribers, feel free to share what you find with your friends who are going through challenging times, or maybe you'll see something that you want to cut out and stick on your refrigerator. If so, go for it! Feel free to write in your book, or to start a companion journal to help you integrate and process what you read. This book is yours to do with as you wish.

My goal is not to present myself as an all-knowing oracle or guru who can save your life by telling you everything you're doing wrong. Rather, my aim is to simply share with you some of my own experiences, mistakes, and fumbles in life, in the hope of giving you useful perspective for whatever you might be going through. Unfortunately (and fortunately), experience is still the best teacher. So while I can't help you avoid the tough lessons, I can at least give you a point of reference that lets you know you aren't the only one having that experience or thinking about life in that way or contemplating those questions.

Speaking of which, as you thumb through these pages and come across stories that you love, make sure you bookmark them so you can revisit them often. And I made sure to include many of my personal favorites. I'm as big a fan of "Light's Daily Dose" as anyone, because I don't take authorship of them—not even of my own personal stories. Meaning, I'm obviously the writer of these 108 "doses," but I have no doubt that they are being channeled through me from the Universe or some higher source. My job over the years has been to show up for the dictation, then transcribe and edit what I hear and feel until it's as close to the source inspiration as possible. Then I know it's ready to be sent out. I honestly cherish each and every one of these doses, and I hope you do too.

My ultimate goal with this book is to help you find and tap into that same source that I've been tapping into for years, and to help you turn up the volume on that source so you can enjoy the same feeling of living your purpose, if you're not already. And by the way, no one can tell you if you're living your purpose or not; only you can know that by the feeling you have in life. To that end, I encourage you to do more than just read the doses. Try to apply the ones that resonate the most. That's how you turn the volume up on your heart and begin living your purpose.

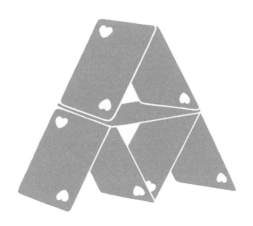

108 Daily
Doses of
Inspiration

e—our *why*. Pe

g their passion an

eaningful action, m

sment, or perhaps

But we could mal

tant days

108 Daily
Doses of
Inspiration

Mark
Twain
famously
said that our two
most important days
in life are the day we are
born and the day we find out
why. But I would add a third day to
that philosophy: the day we start taking
action on our purpose—our *why*. People spend
years contemplating their passion and purpose without ever taking meaningful action, mainly due to fear of
failure, embarrassment, or perhaps self-imposed racism,
ageism, or sexism. But we could make the argument that
out of our three important days, the third day is the
most important. And the best news of all is that our
third day can be *today*. All we have to do is take
one action. A small but meaningful action
step will suffice. This could be doing
some research, or even choosing to
forgo an activity that will free
up time in the days ahead
to build momentum.
What can you do
today to act
on your
why?

WIGGLE ROOM A funny thing happened to me one unusually cold February night in Los Angeles back in 2003. ✦ I was invited by a friend to a talk on meditation given by his meditation teacher, who was visiting from out of town. I decided to go— not because I had any interest in learning meditation—but as a favor to my friend. ✦ If you would've asked me before I walked into the room about my life's purpose, there's a 100 percent chance that my answer wouldn't have had anything to do with meditation. ✦ However, if you asked me the same question after I left that room two hours later, I would've declared that I was destined to become a meditation teacher. ✦ That's the funny (and beautiful) thing about inspiration: there's just no way that we can plan for it. ✦ We may have loose ideas about what we're here to do, and maybe our life is unfolding according to that plan—but there's a decent chance it won't. And the scariest thing about a diversion is not having all the answers. ✦ Even after I knew that becoming a meditation teacher was my calling, there was no vision showing me how it was going to unfold. Remember, this was in 2003, so no one was talking about making a career in meditation at that time. ✦ I kept my day job while continuing to apprentice with my teacher—until one day, about four years after we met, he invited me and a few others to India to train us to become meditation teachers. And the rest is history. ✦ I've learned that this kind of life-altering inspiration can strike at any time—maybe even today. If we have the courage to explore them, our internal hunches have a way of working out for the best. If we ignore them, we may not be able to sleep well at night. ✦ Either way, I recommend leaving a little wiggle room in the long-term plan. Just in case.

SECRET
BEAUTY TIP

for every occasion:
Be generous with your
attention. Really listen when
you're conversing with others.
Encourage the people around you
to be themselves. Show others
that you believe in them. In other
words, make people feel seen.
When they feel seen, the entire world will look more
beautiful to them,
including you.

THE DISCIPLINE ILLUSION "I'm impressed by your discipline," a friend once remarked. "You have a regular meditation practice, you write those daily emails, you don't eat a lot of sweets or drink alcohol. I can't seem to do even one of those things consistently, not to mention all of them together." ✦ "It's an illusion," I told her. "I don't have any more discipline than you. I've failed time and again. I've repeatedly made the common mistake of taking on too much at once, having unrealistic goals, and going cold turkey—only to revert back to my old ways with a vengeance." ✦ The difference comes down to being honest about my strengths and weaknesses, and inserting stopgaps where I know I'm likely to fall short. ✦ For instance, I know I like working out with friends as opposed to by myself, and if I have to get in my car to go work out, I'll likely skip on busy days. So I found a gym with group workouts within walking distance. ✦ Furthermore, I know I have a propensity to overindulge in sweets, so I try not to keep sweets in my house—nor will I grocery shop while hungry, because that's when my resolve is at its weakest. ✦ It took me two years to wean myself off of alcohol after one too many nights of poor sleep and being unproductive the next day. I made the connection and realized it wasn't worth the temporary buzz. ✦ After spending three years writing my first book, I grew so tired of thinking about it that I sent a personal check to a friend for $4,000 with instructions for him to cash it if I didn't finish my final draft by the post-date on the check. That's how I forced myself to finally finish it. I couldn't afford to lose that kind of money. ✦ And finally, when it came to daily meditation, in 2003 I paid someone what was a lot of money to me at the time to teach me how to meditate properly so that I could take the guesswork (and frustration) out of the practice—and now meditation is something I actually look forward to doing twice a day. ✦ So as you see, it's not discipline that I rely upon. It's being realistic about where I am, getting professional help when possible, and understanding what it's going to take to overcome my weaknesses and get to where I want to be.

Something More to Consider: Are you lacking in discipline in certain areas of life? If so, that just means you're normal. Very few people can exercise discipline over long periods of time. Instead of relying on sheer discipline, what else can you do to make engagement with desirable habits more regular? Is it a proximity issue? Could you bring it closer to you so it takes less effort to engage? Can you hire someone to help you understand it better so it feels less confusing? Can you befriend someone to hold you accountable so you have someone else to answer to in addition to yourself? These may not solve all of the problems, but they may help you get enough traction to make the habit stick.

FEED THE BABY Being the parent of an infant or toddler means sacrificing much of what you want to do for what you *have* to do to make sure their needs are met first. ✦ It doesn't matter if you're tired, sick, or traveling—the baby still needs to be fed. And although it's your responsibility to be the provider of food, you're happy to go out of your way to feed your baby because you see that precious little soul as an extension of you. And nothing makes a parent prouder than watching their child grow up to have a positive impact in the world. ✦ I treat these daily messages similarly by mentally keeping them in my "feed the baby" category—meaning, I sacrifice what I want to do (go to bed earlier, sleep in, watch movies) for what I need to do to make sure they are written and sent out on time each day, regardless of how I'm feeling. ✦ Some days are tougher than others, but I rarely see it as a chore. Instead, I treat it as my responsibility because I've realized over the years that they are an extension of me. And nothing makes me prouder than seeing these little stories have a positive impact on people's lives. ✦ If you have a passion project that you'd like to contribute to the world and you're being inconsistent, I highly recommend putting it in the "feed the baby" category so you begin prioritizing it enough for it to take root and grow and create the impact you ultimately want it to have.

Rev. Martin Luther King Jr. was once asked in confidence by a fellow activist whether he thought the 1955 Montgomery bus boycott would actually succeed.

"It is not for me to say or for you to analyze whether I can succeed," he answered.

"My obligation is to do the right thing as I am called upon to do it. The rest is in God's hands."

THE BEST THAT CAN HAPPEN When I was living in New York in the 1990s, I auditioned for an acting conservatory. We had to deliver a monologue and sing a song of our choosing. I chose to sing the hymn "Onward, Christian Soldiers," from my Alabama church days: Onward, Christian So-o-o-oldiers, Marching as to waaaaarrrr, With the cross of Jeeee-sus, Going on befooooooore . . . ✦ I didn't get accepted. I don't know if it was because I couldn't sing, or I wasn't convincing as an actor, or both. ✦ I remember being very nervous and self-conscious during the audition, as a part of me felt like I didn't belong there. Even as I was singing, I cringed at the thought of how awful I probably sounded. ✦ I didn't have the maturity to understand that none of that mattered. Regardless of the circumstances, I was in the room with the director of admissions. I had my shot like anyone else. All I had to do was relax, be myself, and give it my all. ✦ It's normal to feel self-conscious about putting yourself out there. It's also normal to think about the worst that can happen, and to hold back in order to avoid embarrassment, rejection, or public humiliation. ✦ But there's a flip side to that. We can also focus on the best that can happen. And remind ourselves that no matter how unlikely our preferred outcome seems, we have a shot, and if we give it our all and have fun in the process, that's all that counts.

Something More to Consider: First dates, first days at work or school, job interviews, sports competitions, giving speeches, being on the witness stand—these can all be incredibly nerve-wracking experiences. I find that when I make the experience less about me and more about being of service, I'm able to relax more. Of course, meditation and breathwork help too. But it's also good to remember that most people are there to get something from the experience—and if they already had it, then you wouldn't be there. So hone in on whatever value you can provide, and when you are nervous and anxious, just focus on that value. And if you need a little extra help relaxing or getting into the present moment, try taking five to ten deep inhales and exhales *before* going into action.

LOSE MONEY   I don't usually glean a lot of wisdom from Chris Rock movies, but there was one that I watched around 2007 that helped me learn what my priorities were. ✦ Long story short, I had been trying to "flip" properties in Los Angeles as the real estate market was collapsing, and I found myself on the brink of bankruptcy. To make matters worse, my heart was never in real estate. I was an aspiring meditation teacher, but flipping properties looked like an easy way to make a quick buck. ✦ In the movie, Rock's character was married and had a successful career in finance, but he began missing important business meetings due to chasing after a woman behind his wife's back. After his absence eventually caused the firm to lose a big contract, his boss pulled him aside and reasoned: "Look, if you continue to chase after women, you'll always lose money. But if you chase after money, you'll never lose women." ✦ As "off" as it sounds, that line was very profound for me, because it made me realize what I was doing wrong: I had been following his boss's advice and chasing after money. I was so concerned about my future needs being met that I pursued financial opportunities that I wasn't passionate about. And hearing that line gave me a more simplified framework to articulate for myself what was truly important: I replaced "women" with "money," and "money" with "my heart." So the line became, "If I chase after money, I'll always feel disconnected from my heart. But if I chase after what's in my heart, I'll never have to worry about my financial needs being met." ✦ And that was the moment when I decided to relentlessly follow my heart—after watching a bad Chris Rock movie.

THE THING ABOUT ADVICE If you have a deep inner calling to try something that has never been done before—something risky—and you ask someone who's never taken a creative or professional risk before what they think about your idea, there's a good chance that they either are going to tell you not to risk it or will warn you about all the reasons why it will likely result in failure. ✦ But if you ask someone who's taken a healthy amount of professional or creative risks, there's a much higher probability that they'll encourage you to go for it! Because life is short and why live with the regret of not doing what you feel deeply called to do? ✦ The real question is do *you* want to live a life of being risk-averse, or one where you are more inclined to listen to and follow your inner guidance—which, by nature, will lead you off the beaten path? Because the answer to that question will determine whose advice you seek out in the first place.

AN ACT OF KINDNESS During the Holocaust, the Nazis kept the Jews underfed and malnourished to minimize retaliation. As one of the child prisoners fell on the brink of starvation, a Nazi soldier snuck him a rotten potato to eat. The nine-year-old boy credited the soldier's kind gesture with helping him survive the ordeal. ✦ When the boy grew up, he told his son about the Nazi soldier's life-saving deed and the overall importance of showing kindness to others. ✦ In an effort to immortalize his father's touching story and spread the message of kindness, the son created an energy bar in 2004 that became one of the fastest-growing snack brands in the United States. ✦ You've definitely heard of them, and maybe you've even had one: they're called KIND bars.

Something
More to Consider:
I once visited a fast-casual restaurant where I stood in line to order my custom-made salad. When I got up to the register, the checkout person said that my salad was "on the house." Apparently, she had a certain number of "kindness passes" to use with customers, and I was the delighted recipient of one. Maybe you could create something like a kindness pass for you, or for your family, or for your employees to use as well? After all, the only thing better than receiving kindness is giving kindness.

JUST AS REEL One of the reasons we love a good movie is because it exposes our underlying appetite for risk—especially if the hero is putting everything on the line in the name of love or justice or following their heart. ✦ The ensuing drama, the close calls, and surprise endings keep us on the edge of our seat, as we imagine being as brave and selfless as the hero. ✦ Yet, in day-to-day life, we often do the opposite of what we quietly hope our movie heroes do—we go out of our way to avoid risk or ruffle feathers, in the name of playing it safe. ✦ "Ah, that's just in the movies," we rationalize to ourselves. But this is real life, where we have our neat little plans, and the potential negative consequences of veering off of those plans are real. ✦ Perhaps. But we must also remember that there are many positives that can come from following our heart, or taking a leap of faith, or standing up for justice—and those consequences, if they happen, are just as real.

TEACHABLE MOMENTS We are always teaching others how to treat us:

If we are easily reactive, we teach others to sugarcoat their truth.

If we are impartial, we teach people that it's safe to be open and honest with us.

If we routinely gossip about our friends, we teach others to question our loyalty.

If we refuse to spread rumors, we teach people to trust that we will stand up for them too.

If we are reluctant to take responsibility, we teach others to be wary of us playing the victim.

If we own our experience, we teach people to trust that we can shoulder responsibility.

If we consistently over-give, we teach others to take us for granted.

If we give thoughtfully and in accordance to need, we teach people to appreciate our efforts.

If we are perpetually late, we teach others not to depend on us.

If we are punctual, we teach people to respect our time.

Every interaction is a teachable moment. What lessons will you teach today?

ONE STEP AT A TIME One of my favorite stories for dealing with uncertainty is about a prince who was out hunting one cloud-covered afternoon, and while deep in the forest, he lost his way back home. As night fell, the ominous cracks and howls of the forest started closing in, and he began to agonize over his personal safety as well as the safety of those who depended upon him. The prince stood frozen with fear, surrounded by darkness, and unable to orient himself. The sounds of danger inched closer. Something inside told him to just take a single step.

As he did, a pathway mysteriously appeared in the faint moonlight. He doubted if it was even the right direction, and the path went black. His inner guidance urged him to take another few steps, and the pathway reappeared. With each step, the path became brighter, and he realized that it was his movement that was illuminating the way. Eventually, he made it back to safety. When you feel lost, and can't see a clear way out, the best way to determine your next move is to listen to your inner guidance and just follow it one step at a time.

Something more to consider: When you feel lost, or uninspired, or you can't see a path out of a dangerous situation, your tendency may be to freeze with fear so that, at the very least, you don't make the situation worse. But what if the path to greatness is through moving toward the very thing that frightens you? Can you identify something that you are currently afraid of in life and, specifically, something that is standing in the way of where you'd like to go or what you'd like to do? Perhaps it's the uncertainty of leaving a job or doing your job differently? Perhaps it's the thought of going back to school, or having a difficult conversation with a loved one? Whatever it is, we often focus too heavily on the negative aspects of the situation—the worst-case scenarios. But what is the best-case scenario? And what's a way that you can take one small step in that direction?

WILL-STRENGTHENING HARD Ram Dass wrote, "You can do it like it's a great weight on you, or you can do it like it's a part of the dance." ✦ The first time I did a hundred burpees in my fitness class, it felt like the greatest weight. "Why oh why are they having us do this many burpees?" I questioned, as I labored through each set of five repetitions. After about ten minutes, I was dripping with sweat, out of breath, wanting to quit, and only at number fifty. Meanwhile, the others were starting to finish. ✦ A couple minutes later, everyone was done, including this out-of-shape-looking guy and a pregnant lady, while I still had twenty more to go. A few minutes later, the next class showed up, and I still had ten left. I was *dying*. ✦ Then the instructor got down and did the last eight with me, as both classes now waited for me to finish. I was too tired to even be embarrassed at that point. And I think I promised myself that I was never going to do another burpee again. ✦ The next day, I woke up and decided to do a hundred burpees, but this time, on my own—and I would do them like they were a part of a dance. So I put on some music by Fela Kuti and started hopping around. ✦ For some reason, that switch in my mindset made *all* the difference. Don't get me wrong—the burpees were still hard as hell, but it was a different kind of hard. It wasn't that soul-sucking, embarrassing, "when is it going to be over" type of hard that I experienced the day before. But more of an "I *get* to do this," will-strengthening type of hard. And I thoroughly enjoyed strengthening my will. ✦ Today, take something that you've found to be soul-sucking hard and treat it like it's a part of the dance, and see how much it strengthens your will.

A martial arts student went to a teacher
and said earnestly, "I am devoted to
studying your martial arts system.
How long will it take
me to master it?"
The teacher's
reply was
casual:
"Ten
years."
"But what if
I want to master
it faster than that?"
asked the student impatiently.
"I will work very hard. I will practice
every day—ten or more hours a day if I have to.
How long will it take then?" The teacher thought
for a moment, and replied, "Twenty years."

One day in ancient Greece, an acquaintance met with the great philosopher Socrates and said, "Do you know what I just heard about your friend?" ✦ "Hold on a minute," Socrates replied. "Before telling me anything, let's put it through THE TRIPLE FILTER test." ✦ "Triple filter?" ✦ "That's right," Socrates continued. "The first filter is truth. Have you made absolutely sure that what you are about to tell me about my friend is true?" ✦ "No," the man said, "Actually, I just heard about it and—" ✦ "All right," said Socrates. "So you don't even know if it's true. Now let's try the second filter, the filter of goodness. Is what you are about to tell me about my friend something that's good?" ✦ "No, on the contrary—" ✦ "So," Socrates continued, "you want to tell me something bad about him, but you're not certain it's true. Okay, you can still pass the test because there's one filter left: the filter of usefulness. Is what you want to tell me about my friend going to be useful to me?" ✦ "No, not really—" ✦ "Well," concluded Socrates, "if what you want to tell me is neither true nor good nor useful, then why tell it to me at all?"

Something More to Consider: One thing I always try to remember about conversations involving gossip is that anything you say will probably make its way back to the person being talked about. You obviously can't trust a gossipmonger to keep what you say private, so speak *highly* of the person being gossiped about. Give them the benefit of the doubt by defending their actions, or just say, "You know, they can't be all that bad." Those types of responses will make you feel good that you didn't participate in tearing someone down (who you may not even know all that well)—and more importantly, it'll eventually teach the gossip-mongers that you're not the person to bring their gossip to.

THEIR OWN PATH Before he became known for his writing, over a two-year span Eckhart Tolle spent his mornings and afternoons sitting on a local park bench. ✦ He didn't have a plan for what he would do afterward. He literally just sat there, day after day, smiling and enjoying his surroundings. ✦ Imagine how you would feel if your grown brother or son or daughter retreated each morning to the local park, and relaxed on a bench while you headed to work? So it's not surprising that many of Tolle's family members and friends dismissed him as "crazy" and "lazy." ✦ Apparently, the ideas he meditated on while sitting in the park became the basis for his famous book, *The Power of Now*, which made Eckhart Tolle a household name. ✦ In fact, he was once voted the second most influential spiritual person alive, behind the Dalai Lama and ahead of Pope Francis. I'm certain that none of his friends could've imagined that ever happening as he was heading off to the park. ✦ There's so much more to his story than just sitting on a bench, but a key to Tolle's success was undoubtedly occurring while he was being simultaneously dismissed by those closest to him. And this is why we shouldn't be too quick to judge someone else's path simply because they aren't living in the way *we* think they should. ✦ Everyone is walking their own path. Instead of trying to make sense of their actions or worse, ridiculing them, we'd be of far greater use by attempting to understand and support them.

Once
upon a time, a wise
old Sufi was making his annu-
al pilgrimage to Mecca. But it was a
long walk for him, and the sun was high.
Having averaged more than twenty miles a
day, once Mecca was in sight, the old Sufi decided to lie down on the side of the road and rest up
for the final leg of his journey. Minutes later, one of
the other pilgrims violently kicked his feet. "Get up,"
he commanded. "You blasphemer, you lie with your
feet pointed toward God at the holy mosque! What
kind of Sufi are you?" The wise old Sufi cracked
one eye open and said, "I thank you, holy sir.
Now if you would kindly point to a direction
where God is not, I will gladly move my
feet there." ✦ To me, this is the essence
of spirituality. The spiritual person un-
derstands that every place, every
person, every experience, every step, every breath, and
every interaction should
be treated with rev-
erence, that
it's all
God.

THE TEN-YEAR TEST When I was about twenty years old, I missed my grandfather's funeral. ✦ I remember justifying not going because I was extremely busy with college activities, and attending his funeral would've meant having to travel from Washington, DC, back home to Montgomery, Alabama, over a couple of busy school days. ✦ So I opted not to go. ✦ Thinking back, I can't for the life of me remember what occurred over those two school days while my entire family was at the funeral. But I'm sure the memory of attending the funeral would've been stored in my heart forever. ✦ Nowadays, if I have the option to attend a meaningful life event, and I try to convince myself that I'm too busy to go, I counter it by asking myself the following question: if I don't go, will I remember whatever I did instead ten years from now? ✦ If the answer is no, then the choice becomes much easier to make.

THE CRACKED POT A water bearer carried two large clay pots, each hanging on opposite ends of a pole, which he carried to and from a well that was half a mile away. ✦ One pot was cracked, while the other pot appeared smooth and perfect. By the end of the long walk from the well to the house, the cracked pot always arrived half full, while the smooth pot remained full of water. This went on for two years, with the water bearer delivering only one and a half pots of water each day. ✦ Of course, the perfect pot was proud of its accomplishments, while the poor cracked pot felt self-conscious of its own imperfection and ashamed that it was only able to achieve half of what it was designed to do. ✦ While feeling particularly depressed one day, the cracked pot opened up to the water bearer: "I am so ashamed of myself, because this crack in my side causes water to leak out all the way back to your house." ✦ The water bearer laughed, and replied to the pot, "Yes, you leak water, but haven't you noticed the beautiful flowers growing on your side of the path, and not on the other pot's side?" ✦ "That's because I have always known about your flaw, and two years ago, I planted flower seeds on your side of the path, so when I carry you back each day, you water them." ✦ "For two years I have picked these gorgeous flowers to decorate the table. Without you being just the way you are, there would not be this incredible beauty to grace our h

o

m

e.

Several years ago, I decided to run ten laps up this very steep hill around the corner from my house every other day, rain or shine, for a year. To many people, that seemed extreme, but it was the commitment I wanted to make to myself. ✦ On some days, I was running my laps at the crack of dawn, while on other days, I didn't get to my laps until after dinner. I would say that more often than not, I absolutely did not feel like running—but I never once regretted it afterward. ✦ Overall, I learned a lot about commitments that year: I learned that a true commitment isn't ever contingent upon convenience. Otherwise, it's not really a commitment—it's a decision based on current favorable circumstances. ✦ I learned that, with a true commitment, it's hardest to follow through when your schedule gets turned around and no one is there to hold you accountable—but you do it anyway. ✦ I learned that you have to constantly override the part of your mind that wants to excuse you from doing what you said you would do because it's too late, cold, wet, or whatever. And you have to force yourself to listen to that part of you that says, "Look, you don't have to like it, but you're going to do it anyway." ✦ I learned that with a true commitment, you have to constantly replace weak questions that let you off the hook ("Is skipping this once going to kill me?") with stronger questions that render you choiceless ("How can I make it happen today, even though I just want to go to bed?"). ✦ I learned that a true commitment doesn't even start until the original plan goes OUT THE WINDOW.

Something More to Consider: What are you truly committed to right now? And how has your commitment been tested? Look forward to the test, because that's when it becomes cemented as a proper commitment—when it costs you something that you weren't prepared to pay. And remember, you don't have to like the commitment (most people don't) in order for it to be worthy. But it will only get stronger each time you choose to do it anyway.

BOLD IN ACTION Maharishi Mahesh Yogi, the Indian guru and founder of Transcendental Meditation, gathered with his inner circle one afternoon during the very early days of his budding meditation movement. ◆ Maharishi was a celibate with no possessions, yet he spoke in lofty detail about his "world plan" of constructing hundreds of meditation centers in countries around the globe, where thousands of instructors could be trained and dispatched to teach meditation to the masses. ◆ As most of his inner circle nodded in agreement, one brave soul interrupted him with a very sensible question: "But Maharishi, where is the money going to come from to pay for all of this?" ◆ "From wherever it is now," he answered, without even the slightest trace of doubt, and he continued laying out his plan. ◆ True to his word, Maharishi attracted millions in contributions over the years, and trained thousands of teachers who then taught meditation to millions of people around the globe. He demonstrated that the Universe doesn't give us budget-dependent dreams, goals, or visions. ◆ If your dream requires a sizable investment of time, money, and resources, you must operate with absolute confidence that the necessary resources will be generated through your action steps. So be bold in thought, and be just as bold in your actions.

WHILE YOU'RE BUSY There are two kinds of busy—people who are busy trying to do all of the things that are expected of them, and people who are busy doing what's expected of them *plus* a bit extra in order to create a more fulfilling life. ✦ In other words, *everyone* is busy. But the busy people who appear to be thriving (and not just surviving) have likely made a series of consistent and often difficult choices to go the extra mile here, sacrifice comfort there, and budget where possible, in order to stay committed to their dreams. ✦ The big illusion is that life slows down for the successful people more than for others, or that successful people have hidden advantages. But the reality is, successful people are just willing to do *more* than what the average busy person is willing to do. ✦ If you dream of launching a podcast, writing a book, or starting a daily meditation practice, life is not going to slow down in order for you to begin. If you really want it, you're going to have to do it while you're busy.

RESISTANCE The other night, I had to force myself to work out for about the millionth time. One would think that after twenty-plus years of working out, it would be easier to make the time. But on most days, I still have to plead with myself to move. And it's often the same excuses: I'm too tired, I have more important things to do, blah blah blah. ✦ But when I examined my excuse that night, I realized that the solution to my problem was hiding in the excuse: working out would give me the energy I didn't have. It would improve the quality of my sleep. It would strengthen my will the next time I don't feel like working out. ✦ I knew what I had to do. And as is the case 100 percent of the time, I was so glad that I made the effort. But I'll probably resist again in the near future. And hopefully, overcoming my last resistance will make it a tad easier to overcome the next bout of resistance. Wishing you luck with your resistance. And remember, the more you defeat it, the weaker it gets.

The Work

When someone says "I've done the work on myself" (which is a phrase you often hear in places like Los Angeles and Bali), it implies that they've cleared out their past triggers and projections, and they're now accessing their most authentic self. If they're a bit more evolved, they may say, "I'm doing the work," and they may even acknowledge that the process is never-ending. And if they're more evolved than that, they won't say anything about the work, because they'll understand that it doesn't really matter how much work they think they've done or how much they have left to do. The most evolved among us know that what's really happening is the work is being done to us—whether we want it to be or not, whether we're aware of it or not, whether we have the language for it or not. The awareness of it doesn't graduate you from it. It just makes the idea of "the work" slightly easier to accept.

THE WRONG NOTE Pianist Herbie Hancock spent five years as Miles Davis's protegé. During their very first performance together, they were in the moment, playing off each other, improvising. Then Hancock accidentally hit a wrong chord. "It was amazing," Hancock recalled, "Miles is getting to the peak of his solo and then, I played this chord that was so wrong. It was so wrong. I thought I had just, like . . . we had built a house of cards and I just destroyed them all, you know? And Miles just took a breath and then he played some notes that made my chord right." Hancock said that he couldn't figure out how, but Miles somehow fixed his "wrong" note. "It took me years to realize that Miles didn't judge my chord. I did," he said. Later, Miles explained: "It's not the note you play that's the wrong note—it's the note you play afterward that makes it right or wrong."

Something more to consider: As we become more spiritually mature, we understand that while an unintended occurrence may happen at the surface, on a broader spectrum of awareness, there are no mistakes—only learning experiences and growth opportunities. By training yourself to view mistakes this way, you can move into the space of seeing them as opportunities. This will help to minimize any associated ill will and everyone can move past it as quickly as possible. Have you made a mistake lately? Did you try to fix it? Did you get caught in judgment around it? What's one action step you can take now that can make it right?

EVERYTHING AT ONCE   One night after leaving the gym, I stopped by a restaurant to pick up a bowl of soup. The cashier took my order, then—somehow recognzing me—blurted out that he was reading my first book, *The Inner Gym*. ✦ *The Inner Gym* was a five-year labor of love that I self-published and released with practically no marketing. And this was one of the rare times that I crossed paths with a complete stranger who told me he was reading it. I asked where he was in the book, and he said he was on the chapter about gratitude. ✦ It made me realize how much work went into he and I having that one little interaction. We're talking two years of resistance around the idea of writing a book, followed by three-and-a-half years of writing it, in addition to a seemingly endless barrage of edits, second guesses, and rewrites. The only thing that seemed to come easily during the process was the temptation to quit. ✦ But that experience in the café reminded me to send the author some additional words of encouragement. So on my walk home, with my soup in hand, I spoke to my younger self, sitting on the couch in 2013, struggling to complete the book, wanting to give up, and I whispered to him to keep going. I told him you're doing something that will help people, and that the world is waiting. ✦ I believe that everything is happening all at once, and we have the power to transcend the present and inspire our past and future selves. Who knows? Maybe that inner voice we hear sometimes, encouraging us to keep going and not give up, is us—the part of us who has already witnessed the impact of our work. ✦ If you're working on your passion project now, and it's taking you some time to make progress, and you're tempted to give up, try this: the next time you meditate, envision a future moment when you meet someone who was sincerely helped by what you created. Use that image to muster up a little added courage and stamina to see your project through to the end. ✦ And once complete, don't forget to let your younger self know how much it was worth it—and by all means, to keep going, because the world is indeed waiting.

If you have no idea how you ended up wherever you are, welcome to the club. The truth is, none of us can really know what's going on by looking at whatever's happening (or not happening) right now. We may think we know what this phase of life is all about, but it won't be until much later that we can see what it was *really* about. For now, we must keep trusting that we're right where we're supposed to be, going through whatever we need to be experiencing (for all reasons). We don't need to understand the hows and whys right now because we're still moving through it and none of us can see the forest for the trees. We certainly don't want to get caught up in judging this tree as a waste of time and that tree as a mistake, or we may completely miss the point: they're all growth opportunities, SHAPED LIKE TREES.

Something More to Consider: Are you going through a confusing time right now, where you feel lost, turned around, hopeless? It's sometimes hard to see a purpose to the suffering, loneliness, or inner turmoil. But when we study the biographies of those who've also experienced great adversity, it's hard not to see that even still, the Universe was delivering a gift to them—in the form of learning, a growth opportunity, or a means of discovering their higher purpose. When you get a moment, look up the biographical sketch of any noteworthy figure from the past, and there's an excellent chance that you will discover that their life was not just bumpy but riddled with rejection, loss, and despair. You'll also see how those very same rejections prepared them for their biggest successes. And if they could stay the course, so can you.

FURTHER DOWN THE ROAD There's a plot twist in one of my favorite books, *The Alchemist*, where the hero is on a treasure hunt and gets beaten up pretty badly by some thieves. They rob him of everything and leave him stranded on the side of the road, where he eventually falls asleep. ✦ Later in the story, we find out that if the mugging didn't happen right when it did, which led to him falling asleep, the hero would've likely been murdered by a deranged killer who was awaiting his next victim further down the road. So as it turns out, getting mugged ended up saving the hero's life. ✦ A trademark of the Universe is to use unanticipated rejection as protection from something much worse. And that's where trust comes in. Trust that if you do your absolute best, and you're still being rejected, or delayed, or even mugged, it likely means you're being protected from something worse that was hiding further down the road. In other words, the Universe is always conspiring for you.

Did
you
know
that all
humans
alive today
are related—
meaning we all
come from the
same unbroken
line of humans? ✦
Researchers have
even pinpointed the
woman who is our
great-grandmother to
the power of 700. She
lived between 152,000 and
234,000 years ago. And our
great-great-great-great-great-
great-great-great-great-great- . . .
granddaddy supposedly lived between
200,000 and 300,000 years ago as well.
✦ This means that you and I, and everyone
on the freeway, and in the office building, and
on TV, are cousins. Literally, everyone we will
come into contact with in life is our distant rela-
tive. Let's remember that as we go about our day,
and treat one another less like strangers and more like
what we actually are: family. WELCOME TO THE FAMILY

AUTOCORRECTT When we write, if we get it wrong because we were preoccupied or tired, our devise gives us the benefit of the doubt. The devise knows that, based on our past behavior, we probably didn't mean to type bannana, so it suggests banana. ✦ The reason it's difficult two communicate via speech is because theirs no delete function, no autocorrect, and very little benefit of the doubt—unless one is mature enough to understand that the nature of speech is first draft, and that tired or preoccupied people don't always communicate effectively. ✦ Just to be clear, I'm not suggesting that anyone except verbal abuse or gaslighting. But everyone slips up and says something they don't meen from time to time. So be willing to at least ask if that's what they meant to say. And if it wasn't, then forgiveness is nature's autocorrect.

DREAMS DEFERRED I once heard an interesting story of a man who started a foundation to work with late-stage cancer patients by helping them fulfill whatever dreams they had buried for years or decades because life got too busy, or they were too focused on pleasing others, or they were pursuing more serious endeavors. ✦ As they continued their cancer treatment, this would be a final chance for each to express what was in their heart while there was still a bit of time left. ✦ He helped one cancer patient begin painting, and organized guitar lessons for a man who had always wanted to play but never did. He helped another patient finally start the garden she'd always fantasized about creating, while another enrolled in dance lessons. ✦ Over time, many patients began showing signs of remission, and some lived on for years cancer-free. In other words, their immune systems began positively responding to their renewed enthusiasm for doing the simple things that brought them joy. ✦ Society doesn't teach us that the little creative impulses inside matter as much as striving for comfort and material success—but depending on how we define ultimate "success," making space in our busy lives to explore those little impulses could literally be one of the healthiest ways to spend our time.

HOW TO HELP We've all heard the saying, "Stay away from negative people—they have a problem for every solution." But here's the thing: some people may not be interested in *our* solutions to their problems. ✦ I remember back when I was a hard-core vegan, every conversation I had about health would end with me trying to convince the other person that they needed to become vegan, or shaming them for not already being vegan. You know the joke: how do you know someone is vegan? They'll tell you after about thirty seconds. Well, that was me. I wouldn't shut up about it.

And then one day, I was speaking with a good friend of mine about the fact that he was tired, and I suggested that the reason he was tired was probably because he wasn't vegan. And he shouted, "Going vegan isn't the answer to everybody's problem!" It was shocking, because I didn't realize how insistent I was being, and it taught me to let people find their own way, just like I found my way. The irony is, I'm not even vegan anymore. ✦ The bottom line is this: even though our intentions are generally good, we have to know when it's appropriate to offer help, and when it's best to allow other people to figure things out for themselves. Or, to know that now may not be the time or place for our suggestion. Maybe the solution has to be *their* idea, and not ours. These are the same considerations that we would want people to make before trying to help us, so why not make them for others? Maybe that becomes our opportunity—not to write anybody off as "negative" or "uncoachable" but to help them by exercising a little more patience and understanding.

ONE BIKE LEFT The difference in how men think versus women: Once, I was facilitating a retreat in Tulum, Mexico, and my girlfriend and I wanted to go for a bike ride. But the resort only had one bike left for rent. So we decided to share the bike—she would ride on the handlebar while I peddled. ✦ Later, we passed by a friend of mine from New York, who was out riding separate bikes with his new wife. The four of us stopped and chatted for a while, then we continued on our separate ways. ✦ As I peddled away, I nudged my girlfriend on the handlebar, and said, "You know, I'll bet that guy was thinking how I'm a cheap bastard for not spending the extra money to rent you your own bike." ✦ My girlfriend's reply was, "That's funny, because I was just thinking how romantic his wife probably found it that we chose to ride on the same bike."

Something More to Consider: This is a classic example of how men and women can process the same situation completely differently. Many times, when we are in disagreement, it's because the man is viewing the situation from his male brain, and the woman from her female brain. Instead of arguing over whose perspective is correct, see where you can find unity in your *values*. If you both want the same things (to be happy, to feel safe, to save money), it may be easier to arrive at a consensus that way.

THE REAL REASON When people start asking why a past relationship or former job didn't work out, it's not really a fair question because we're then expected to compress months' or years' worth of life experience, expectations, miscommunications, false assumptions, and sincere intentions into a couple of sentences. ✦ The sensational reason we often give is rarely the real reason. That is to say, it's not the underlying reason that most things in life come to an end. ✦ It's also not as interesting to share the real reason, because it's practically the same reason we left middle school, high school, and perhaps college: we learned what we came to learn, our studies were complete, and it was time to move on.

NEW YEARS Last New Year's Eve, I posted the following on my social media page: *This year is going to be as difficult as last year, no matter what you're intending to create.* ✦ If you're still defining a "good" year by manifesting comfort and material success, you'll be setting yourself up for profound disappointment year after year. ✦ If you can view the years like college courses, and expect them to be challenging and difficult, you'll be better prepared to engage in the process of learning. ✦ If you got broken up with or fired this past year, it wasn't a "bad" year if those experiences helped you develop more valuable tools for loving yourself, or for making better life choices, or for honoring your boundaries. ✦ Learning these kinds of lessons is not a pretty or comfortable process, and it sometimes involves dark nights of the soul and lots of tears. But that's how we learn. No one learns anything of value while comfortable. ✦ So forget about creating more comfort in this coming year. Instead, cherish the challenges, and look forward to your upcoming lessons as a master class in self-love—and judge this next year by how many wonderful life lessons you were able to learn. ✦ If the year doesn't stretch you, you won't learn anything new, and you're just going to have to repeat that class the following year.

EVERY LITTLE BIT COUNTS I once went on a Jack the Ripper walking tour through East London, and what I found more shocking than the details of the murders were the horrific living conditions in late nineteenth-century London. ✦ There was essentially no running water in that part of town, which was full of immigrants living in filthy tenements. People would only bathe about once a month (at a bathhouse), and while at home, they would use the bathroom in a bucket and dump the excrement out of their window onto the streets below, where children were often playing barefoot. There was no way to wash their hands or feet when they came inside, so many children died of typhoid fever before the age of five. Apartments had poor ventilation and were infested with cockroaches and rats. Eighty-five percent of the women were prostitutes, and most people had STDs and were borderline alcoholics, and so on. ✦ I thought, wow, we've really come a long way as a society. And what's interesting is, a hundred years from now, I'll bet that people will look back with equal amounts of shock at the number of homeless people we have, the mental health crisis that we mostly ignore, the masses of people we let die from senseless gun violence, and the number of black and brown people we unjustly lock up in our prisons—and they'll think, wow, we've come so far as a society. And, they will undoubtedly have their issues that seem impossibly difficult to solve. ✦ I guess what I'm trying to say is, as bad as things seem now, they are a big improvement from where we were a hundred years ago. With humans, change is very much a cumulative effect, where even the smallest acts of kindness are helping to move things along. And as insignificant as our actions may seem today—recycling, going strawless, sharing information about local injustices—trust that every bit counts. Keep fighting, keep praying, keep giving, and keep being grateful for what you have. Positive change is so steady that we barely even notice it.

Dear Lord, so far today, I am doing all right!
I haven't been greedy, mean, selfish, nasty,
self-indulgent, gossiped or lost my temper.
I have not complained, whined, cursed, or
eaten any chocolate, nor have I charged
anything to my credit card. But . . .
I'll be getting out of bed in a
minute, and I'm really going
to need your help then.

THE LIFE MAMMOGRAM When my mother came home from getting her first mammogram, she called me and, with her usual dry sense of humor, described the experience like this: "As the mammogram machine flattened out my breast, at first it felt uncomfortable, then slightly painful. But it kept going, slowly flattening it out more and more, and still more. And every time I thought, "Okay, it's not possible for my breast to get any flatter," the machine flattened it even more." ✦ Fortunately, she got a clean bill of health. Yet her description reminds me of what happens to us sometimes in life—when we occasionally get subjected to long periods of suffering, where it feels like we're being emotionally stretched more and more. And just when we think, "Okay, my suffering can't get any worse than this," we get stretched even more. ✦ Like the mammogram, we are being stretched for our own good. Instead of looking for signs of cancer, the "life mammogram" exposes the aspects of our ego that may be the cause of our suffering. You know, the part of us that is afraid—afraid of failure, afraid of what others may think about us, afraid of losing what we've built, afraid of not finding love. ✦ Meanwhile, being stretched gives our spirit a glorious opportunity to shine through and remind us of who we truly are—not the human having a spiritual experience, but a fearless, omnipotent spirit having the humbling human experience.

THE ANSWER The greatest gift you can ever give to yourself is the gift of taking full responsibility for your life. Because if you and you alone are responsible for how things have ended up, then the answer to turning things around is also right there in the room with you.

EVERYTHING IS AN ILLUSION A devotee heard his guru say that everything in life was an illusion. On his way home, the man saw a wild elephant stampeding through a small village. He stood frozen with fear as the elephant began coming in his direction. ✦ Everyone ducked and dove out of the way. A shopkeeper saw the devotee standing in the middle of the road and yelled for him to move out of the way of the elephant. But remembering what his beloved guru said about everything being an illusion, he thought, perhaps this is his guru's way of testing his faith—the elephant is probably an illusion. ✦ A few seconds later, the elephant trampled the man pretty badly, sending him to the hospital. When the guru came to check on him, the devotee grew very angry. "I thought you said that everything in life was an illusion! But that elephant was real!" ✦ "The elephant actually *was* an illusion," retorted the wise guru, "and so was that shopkeeper who warned you to get out of the way."

Something more to consider: Imagine if you were floating in orbit around the Earth and looking down at the vast blue ocean. From that high up, you wouldn't be able to make out any of the ocean's individual waves. In fact, from that high up, the ocean would appear rather stagnant, not fluid. But to someone swimming in the ocean, it would feel anything but stagnant. If both parties reported on what the nature of the ocean was—stagnant or fluid—who would be correct? Both. The ocean is both stagnant *and* fluid at the same time, depending on your vantage point. Similarly, saying life is both real *and* an illusion depends on which vantage point you're referring to—from the spiritual perspective or from the ground-level perspective? One perspective doesn't cancel out the other. Instead, they complement one another. The spiritual perspective reminds us that everything is connected, while the ground-level perspective allows us to be fully immersed in the human experience. The idea is to live both simultaneously.

YOUR ATTITUDE Miles Davis said, "Anybody can play. The note is only 20 percent. The attitude of the motherfucker who plays it is 80 percent." ✦ This is why it doesn't matter if someone else has done the same thing you want to do. They may be technically proficient, but they are not you. They don't have your life experience. They don't have your unique perspective. They don't share your motivation. They haven't been on your path, nor have they had to overcome the challenges you've overcome. This is what creates your style, your attitude, your swagger. When you bring all of that into the room, it'll be yours and no one else's.

Dear Sounds True friend,

Since 1985, Sounds True has been sharing spiritual wisdom and resources to help people live more genuine, loving, and fulfilling lives. We hope that our programs inspire and uplift you, enabling you to bring forth your unique voice and talents for the benefit of us all.

We would like to invite you to become part of our growing online community by giving you three downloadable programs—an introduction to the treasure of authors and artists available at Sounds True! To receive these gifts, just flip this card over for details, then visit us at **SoundsTrue.com/Free** and enter your email for instant access.

With love on the journey,

TAMI SIMON   Founder and Publisher, Sounds True

SOUNDS TRUE
many voices, one journey   800.333.9185

ST330

Real Meditation doesn't look anything like the photos you see online, of people sitting perfectly erect on cushions in brightly-lit whitewashed rooms, or atop cliffsides overlooking a ravine. Real meditation happens in living rooms with little people walking around banging on ~~this~~ things. It happens in the closet after a fight with your spouse. It happens in the car while parked on a busy street, before going into the bar for drinks with friends. Real meditation gets interrupted by the neighbor watching Wheel of Fortune too loud, or the dog barking at a squirrel. Real Meditation involves drool, and sleep, and farts, and bizarre thoughts about armadillos. Real meditation is spontaneous and cluttered. Internet meditation happens only when the camera is on. Real meditation **happens** when nobody is watching.

SO GULLIBLE People think meditation makes you gullible, but it's actually stress that makes you gullible. Stress makes you crave french fries, cookies, and wine. Stress makes you come up with important-sounding excuses about why you can't exercise. Stress makes you think the reason you're tossing and turning at night is because you don't have the right mattress. Stress keeps you locked in codependent relationships with emotionally unavailable partners. Stress makes you say and do foolish things you have to apologize for later. Stress even makes you think you're incapable of meditating (because your mind is too busy). ✦ Meanwhile, meditation makes you bold. Meditation makes it really hard to put up with someone else's BS. Meditation makes it almost impossible to remain at a dead-end job or in a bad relationship. Meditation makes you stand up for others and follow your heart with no fallback plan. Meditation allows you to be guided by your intuition instead of your fear. Meditation helps you accept others and let go of the need to control. Meditation helps you sleep like a baby, even though you don't have it all figured out.

Wanna try a one-minute meditation? Just sit in a relaxed position, close your eyes, and take a five-second inhale, counting to yourself, followed by a five-second exhale. Repeat for five more cycles in a row, and after the last cycle, slowly open your eyes. Even though it's only a minute long, if you're feeling anxious or unfocused, doing this quick meditation can provide you with a surprisingly powerful reset.

WHAT FEELS RIGHT An old man, a boy, and a donkey were heading into town. The boy rode on the donkey while the old man walked. As they went along, people remarked that it was a shame for the old man to be walking and the boy to be riding. The man and boy thought maybe the critics were right, so they switched positions.

Later, they passed some people who remarked, "What a shame, a grown man makes that little boy walk." So they both decided to walk. Soon they passed more people who thought they were stupid to walk when they had a donkey to ride. So, they both rode the donkey.

Next, they passed some people who shamed them by saying how awful it was to put such a load on a poor donkey. No matter what you do or how you do it, there will be people who have an opinion about it. Since you obviously can't please everyone, err on the side of doing what feels right to you.

Something More to Consider: There's a saying that I like to remember whenever I receive criticism: *You will never be criticized by people who are doing more than you—only by those who are doing less.* And it's so true. The loudest critics are usually the spectators who are watching comfortably from the sidelines. Those taking action don't have time to critique you because they're too busy fulfilling their own dreams. And true leadership requires that you withstand the criticism while staying focused on your dream.

THE
POWER TO HEAL

A sage was walking past a village one day and was beckoned by a woman to help a sick child nearby. ✦ As the concerned sage approached, a crowd gathered around—for such a man was a rare sight. ✦ The sage began to pray over the sick child. ✦ "Do you really think your prayer will help when medicine has failed?" barked a skeptic from the crowd. ✦ "You know nothing of such things," replied the sage to the man. "You're just an ugly, stupid idiot!" ✦ The man's face grew red-hot at these words. He was about to lash out when the sage came over to him and said calmly: "If one sentence has the power to make you so angry, might not a prayer have the power to heal?" ✦ And thus, the sage healed two people that day. ✦ Treat your words as the mighty instruments they are—to heal, to bring into being, to nurture, to cherish, to bless, and to forgive.

THE GRATITUDE CONVERSATION Telling a loved one who worries a lot to "stop worrying" is like telling them to stop being hungry. It doesn't work like that, and it may cause them to worry even more. ◆ If you genuinely want to help someone calm down, when the time is right, try asking them this question: What are you grateful for in this moment? If they don't have an answer, say, "Well, I'm grateful for this about you," and tell them something specific that you genuinely appreciate about them. ◆ Worrying comes from a fear of the future, whereas gratitude leads us back to the present moment. So in a way, this type of gratitude conversation can be a solution for connection and for helping someone to calm their nerves without ever having to tell them to "calm down."

DIFFERENT DEFINITIONS I once had a yoga instructor proclaim that the headstand is the most spiritual yoga pose we could ever do. ✦ As a former yoga teacher, I remember thinking to myself, "Is this guy an idiot? How do you determine which yoga pose is the *most* spiritual?" ✦ And then it hit me: *his* definition of "spiritual" and my definition of "spiritual" are probably different. His is based on his life experiences and training, and mine is based on my experiences. ✦ Later, I began to see a pattern: whenever I would get upset with someone for saying something that I thought was stupid, it was often because we had different definitions for the same words or ideas. ✦ Common words like "punctual," "thoughtful," "loving," "spiritual," "safe," can mean completely different things to different people! ✦ I realized that if I spent less time rejecting people because I didn't agree with them, and more time understanding how they defined concepts like "love," "happiness," and "connection," I would discover that we often desired the same things.

ABUNDANCE I have a friend whose mother packed her school lunch every day when she was in first grade. My friend's mom eventually learned that my friend had been giving away half of her lunch to another first-grader whose parents couldn't afford packed lunches. ◆ Instead of berating the child for sharing her only sustenance, my friend's mother began sending her to school with two lunches—one for her, and one for her classmate. ◆ As the child selflessly and abundantly shared what she had, she received even more of it to give, even without asking for it or trying to manifest it. This is the essence of reciprocity. It comes from abundant behavior, and not merely from wishful thinking.

TO THE MOUNTAINTOP

As I mentioned earlier, every other day for a year I ran hill sprints in my old neighborhood in Los Angeles. ✦ It was a long hill, and my plan was always the same: sprint as fast as I could to the halfway point, stop, then walk back down to the bottom of the hill, and repeat for a total of ten laps. ✦ Well, one morning, as I was in the middle of my eighth lap, I heard the rattle of a shopping cart echoing from further up the hill. ✦ I finished my lap at the usual halfway mark (as I had done hundreds of times before), and the man pushing his cart down the hill pointed behind him to the top and yelled out in a raspy, half-drunken voice, "God said to go all the way to the *top* of the mountain! He didn't say, go halfway up and then quit!" ✦ His sarcastic commentary was actually funny, but it also reminded me of how well-meaning people sometimes offer unsolicited advice without first taking the time to understand what our overall goal is. ✦ The advice can even be sound or poignant, but if they don't appreciate what we're trying to achieve, then it may be the wrong advice for our circumstances—yet we may feel an obligation to follow it. ✦ I say this because the old me would've deviated from the plan on my last two laps just to appease the man with the shopping cart, who was now watching to see if I would run to the top. ✦ Instead, I kindly invited him to sprint those last two laps with me to show me how to go to the top of the mountain—and as expected, he declined.

Something
More to Consider:
Are you following your
path, or someone else's path
for you? No one can tell you which
path you're supposed to take in life.
Most people can't even see their own path,
much less yours. I love how Joseph Campbell put
it: "If you can see your path laid out in front of you step
by step, you know it's not your path. Your own path you
make with every step you take. That's why it's your path."

TWENTY-SEVEN YEARS Nelson Mandela spent twenty-seven years in prison. Confined to a small cell without a bed or plumbing, he was forced to do hard labor in a quarry. He could write and receive a letter once every six months, and once a year he was allowed to meet with a visitor for only thirty minutes. After Mandela's release, he famously said: "As I walked out the door toward the gate that would lead to my freedom, I knew if I didn't leave my bitterness and hatred behind, I'd still be in prison."

The misconception of this story is that people think Mandela suddenly became forgiving on the day he was released. But he's human, and I imagine he wrestled with his ability to forgive his captors long before his release, especially when there was no hope of being released. When we find ourselves moving through trying moments, and particularly if a situation appears hopeless, that's when our practice of love, forgiveness, and compassion can have the most impact on our inner growth—and that's why

we must continually redirect our attention onto the higher lessons being learned, not the means by which they are being learned. We should assume that if we're stuck in

something dreadful, and we can't get out, then we're learning something that will help us mine our own greatness—something we will perhaps one day use to help and inspire

others. From a spiritual perspective, I would offer that it took Mandela twenty-seven years to learn how to be completely and unconditionally forgiving. And once he fully

embodied it, he was released from prison. And that was a large part of what made him the great man whose words and principles we love to quote and emulate today.

OUR WORDS AND ACTIONS Prayer doesn't have to be a singularly religious act conducted on our knees with our palms pressed together while imagining that we're engaged in a one-on-one with the divine. A prayer can also be as simple as an act of gratitude—a "thank you" to a neighbor, a smile to a stranger, an "I appreciate you" to a spouse. Yes, these are prayers too. Because if we could somehow see beyond the flesh, we might be shocked to realize that this entire time, we've been in constant contact with the divine through our everyday words and actions.

It took me twenty-five years to attend my first yoga class, and nearly thirty years to start meditating with consistency. ✦ If you would've told me in college that I would be a professional meditation teacher in my forties, I would have laughed you out of my dorm room. It was actually a chain-smoking DJ who inspired me to start practicing yoga many years later, and that led me to meditation. ✦ I believe we all have the capacity to change—but on our terms. And the angels who are sent to inspire us to change are often cast against type. It could literally be anyone—the Uber driver, our passive-aggressive boss, the barista, our estranged sibling. ✦ So if we're frustrated because someone we care about isn't doing what we feel they should be doing today in order to better themselves, it doesn't mean they are lost or that we know what's best for them. If we could pull the lens back far enough, we would see that they are actually RIGHT ON TIME—their time, not ours.

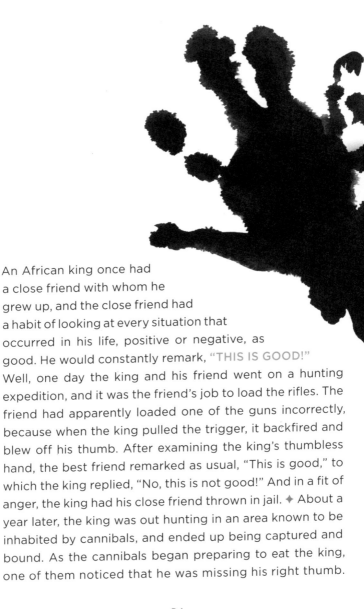

An African king once had
a close friend with whom he
grew up, and the close friend had
a habit of looking at every situation that
occurred in his life, positive or negative, as
good. He would constantly remark, "THIS IS GOOD!"
Well, one day the king and his friend went on a hunting
expedition, and it was the friend's job to load the rifles. The
friend had apparently loaded one of the guns incorrectly,
because when the king pulled the trigger, it backfired and
blew off his thumb. After examining the king's thumbless
hand, the best friend remarked as usual, "This is good," to
which the king replied, "No, this is not good!" And in a fit of
anger, the king had his close friend thrown in jail. ✦ About a
year later, the king was out hunting in an area known to be
inhabited by cannibals, and ended up being captured and
bound. As the cannibals began preparing to eat the king,
one of them noticed that he was missing his right thumb.

Being superstitious, they never ate anyone who was less than whole. So they set him free. ✦ As he returned home, the king realized that his dear friend was right after all—getting his thumb accidentally blown off was indeed a good thing. ✦ He immediately freed his old friend from prison, apologizing profusely and telling him all that happened with the cannibals. "I am very sorry for sending you to jail for so long," he said remorsefully. "It was not right for me to do that, and I hope that someday you can forgive me." ✦ "No no no," his friend interrupted, "this is very good!" ✦ "This is not good!" the king snapped. "You have to stop saying that! How could sending my best friend to jail for a year possibly be good?" ✦ "No, it is good," replied the friend. "Because if I had not been in jail, I would have been in the cannibal village with you."

Something More to Consider: Are you currently experiencing a situation that you've labeled as "bad?" If so, there's a chance that you're limiting the possibilities of what that situation can lead to simply by having a negative attitude about it. What if you were forced to think of five positive lessons, outcomes, or opportunities that could come from the most recent "bad" situation you've experienced. What would they be? ✦ I've also shared this story when leading group meditations to illustrate how we should treat our busy minds. Instead of seeing some thoughts as bad and others as good, it's more helpful to adopt the best friend's attitude and see all thoughts as good in meditation. In other words, embracing all of your thoughts is the secret to stilling the mind.

IN A WORLD-CLASS WAY Back when I lived in New York and Whole Foods had just opened on Seventh Avenue, it was like an amusement park—they needed about twenty registers and five roped-off lanes just to shuttle all the customers through the checkout process. ✦ If you were there in those days, you might remember seeing a tall, stately, African American gentleman who stood in the front of the checkout line, directing the customer traffic. When your turn came, he would point to you and call out your register number with the baritone cadence of a boxing ring announcer. He was so smooth, it was like watching an artist at work. ✦ I can't imagine that his job would've paid very much. But he treated it as though he was the maestro of Whole Foods, gracefully directing customers to their designated register. His massive presence commanded the respect of everyone in line—so he rarely had to get anyone's attention, because you were already paying attention to him.

✦ Anyway, many months later, I saw a familiar face on the cover of the *New York Times*. It was a profile on the lane announcer from Whole Foods! Some reporter had been so mesmerized by how masterfully he performed his job that she was inspired to profile him in the paper. ✦ Now, he could've just been some guy who was hired to call out register numbers—you know, not really wanting to be there, mailing it in, treating the job like it was beneath him. But instead, this wonderful man chose to be the maestro of Whole Foods—the man who people would be delighted to stand in a long line to see and hear. And God knows what sorts of amazing opportunities came from that *New York Times* write-up. ✦ Bottom line: we may not currently work at a world-class job or in a world-class environment, but if we treat whatever we do in a world-class way, the right people will notice, and the work opportunities we ultimately dream about will be much more likely to come.

THE OPPOSITE In the popular sitcom *Seinfeld* there's a classic episode where George Costanza remarks to Jerry how he thinks every decision he's made in life has been wrong, and as a result, his life has turned out to be the opposite of what it should've been. ✦ So Jerry advises him to start doing the opposite of what he would normally do in every situation. And when the perpetually single and broke George follows this advice, sure enough, his life turns around—he meets the woman of his dreams, he finally moves out of his parents' house, he lands a lucrative job with the Yankees, and so on. ✦ Even though it's just a sitcom, Jerry's suggestion of trying the opposite can actually apply in real life too—especially if we feel like we're forcing things to happen, such as trying to make a broken relationship work, close a deal, or get someone to like you. ✦ What's often called for is not more control, but the opposite: *letting go*. Let go of your attachment to the outcome. Let go of the timing. Of course, keep being yourself and doing your best, but operate more from a space of abundance instead of scarcity. ✦ And like George, you might not get exactly what you wanted. You might attract something even better.

Something More to Consider: Are you forcing something right now? Remember, letting go doesn't mean giving up. It just means switching tactics. Maybe trying a different approach, and becoming less outcome-oriented and more process-oriented. It's like weight-lifting. If you're straining on your very first repetition, you're probably going too heavy, which means you're also risking injury. Instead, back off a little. Go lighter. Figure out a way to keep it challenging, but doable.

There's a way to be OUTSTANDING without having degrees, titles, money, or anything other than what you have on you right now. It's very simple: just do what you say you're going to do. ✦ If you say you're going to be somewhere at a certain time, show up at that time. If you say you're going to finish something by a certain date, finish it by then. If you say you're going to start a new habit, then start that habit and commit to it. ✦ These days, it's become such a rare thing for people to actually do what they say they're going to do, that following through on your word repeatedly and with enthusiasm will start to make you really stand out from the crowd.

I
once
took a live-figure
drawing class at New York
University, which started out on the first
day with the teacher giving us only ten seconds
to draw a pose. We were all feverishly sketching away when, seconds later, he quietly announced, "PENCILS DOWN." ✦ He then instructed the model to switch positions and gave us twenty seconds to draw the new pose. We were in slightly less of a panic. ✦ The model changed positions again, and the teacher gave us a full minute, which felt like all the time in the world. ✦ For the main pose, we had twenty minutes. I could've drawn *The Last Supper* in detail. ✦ The teacher knew that if he started off by giving us twenty minutes, we would've likely wasted much of our time getting caught up in the minutiae and then rushed to finish near the end. ✦ Instead, he showed us how an artfully imposed set of deadlines could help us stretch out the time and avoid potential creative blocks. ✦ Have you found yourself creatively stuck lately? If so, try giving yourself a shorter-than-reasonable deadline as a way of igniting your creative juices. For instance, if you have a week to complete a creative project, experiment with what happens if you only gave yourself forty-eight hours to complete it. The additional sense of urgency may help you access a level of creativity you didn't even know was there. Creating art is a lot like conversing. It needs to flow. The more time you have to think about it, the more mechanical and cagey it can feel.

THE BEAUTY OF DREAMS Once, after speaking at a conference, I was running late to the Vancouver airport. We were being driven from Whistler and found ourselves inching across the historic Lions Gate Bridge in heavy traffic. Contemplating whether I would make my flight, I glanced outside from the back seat of the car and saw a little handwritten note taped to one of the rails near the peak of the bridge. I could barely make out what it said, so I took a photo and enlarged it. The note read: "The future belongs to those who believe in the beauty of their dreams," which I learned later was a quote by Eleanor Roosevelt. But not knowing the source, I immediately began thinking of the person who created it, and I wondered who or what inspired them to handwrite it, and then tape it right there at the top of the bridge? And who was the intended audience? ✦ Was it for someone who might be standing at the top of the bridge, thinking of jumping? Was it to lift the mood of drivers stuck in traffic? Then the moment passed and I forgot about it. ✦ As I sat in the airport later, scrolling through my camera roll, I came across the photo of the note, and thought, what if it was intended for someone who writes a daily inspirational message . . . who would be stuck in traffic on that day, at that spot . . . who might one day write a book and share this message with people around the world? We'll never know, but it goes to show how far and wide these little gestures of kindness can spread when we're paying attention.

The
future
belongs to
those who
believe
in the
beauty
of their
dreams.

FREE AT LAST I saw a brilliant documentary called *King in the Wilderness*, about Dr. Martin Luther King Jr.'s last years, which were his most trying, both personally and professionally. ✦ His approval rating was dismal, and he had been abandoned by many supporters after he began speaking out against poverty and the war in Vietnam. ✦ Singer Harry Belafonte, who was one of Dr. King's confidants, recalled how during that final year Dr. King had developed a slight tick—possibly from the constant emotional and psychological pressure he lived under; and how, many months later, he noticed that Dr. King's tick had mysteriously disappeared. ✦ He mentioned his observation to Dr. King, who acknowledged that his tick had indeed gone away. When Belafonte asked how he got rid of it, Dr. King told him that he had made his peace with death. ✦ Dr. King was assassinated in Memphis, Tennessee, not long after that conversation, at only thirty-nine years old. ✦ Another close friend of Dr. King's, Andrew Young, mentioned a similar sentiment that was shared with him in the months leading up to the assassination. He remembered Dr. King saying that in order to be truly free, one *must* overcome the love of wealth and the fear of death.

BIG MISTAKE When I was about thirteen, I decided to experiment with cutting my own hair instead of going to the barber. I had a little afro because that was the style back in the 1980s. Well, I forgot to put the guard on the clippers, and within fifteen seconds I had cut a big plug into my hair, all the way down to the scalp. ✦ After spending five minutes trying to figure out how to reverse time, I reluctantly cut all of my hair off, exposing my pale scalp and my huge, protruding ears. I was so embarrassed that I skipped school the next day in the hope that my hair would grow back enough for people not to notice. ✦ Looking back, I realized that cutting a big plug in my hair was my most important lesson in becoming a barber—because I never forgot the guard again, and I got so good at it that I never visited a barbershop again. ✦ Whenever we try something new or step outside of our comfort zone, the initial mistakes and ensuing embarrassment come with the terrain. They are often the unforgettable lessons, which makes them necessary for achieving mastery.

A LITTLE MORE COURAGE

Bravery isn't about being fearless. It's about loyalty. If we are loyal to our heart, we will find our courage. And while we may still be petrified, as long as we have a little more courage than we have fear, we can take action.

THE SHIPWRECK The only survivor of a shipwreck washed up on a small, uninhabited island. He prayed feverishly for God to rescue him, and every day he scanned the horizon for help, but none seemed forthcoming.

He eventually managed to build a little hut out of driftwood to protect him from the elements and to store his few remaining possessions.

But one day, after foraging for food, he arrived back to find his little hut in flames, the smoke billowing up to the sky. The worst had happened; everything was lost. The man was stung with grief and anger. "I've lost so much already! How could God do this to me?" he cried.

Early the next day, he was awakened by the sound of a ship that was approaching the island. It had come to rescue him. "But how did you know I was here?" asked the weary man of his rescuers. "We saw your smoke signal."

Even when it looks like the worst has happened, trust that it's always happening for you—not to you.

BOTH-AND "I *would* follow my heart, but I've got to pay the bills . . ." ★ "If only I had more money, I could spend more time volunteering . . ." ★ "My kids take up all of my time, so I really don't have the energy to work on my passion project . . ." ★ But real life is more of a "both-and" than an "either-or." ★ Both-and keeps you committed to your dreams and passions, no matter what else is happening. Either-or will keep letting you off the hook.

Something More to Consider: Sometimes, we get intimidated by the thought of taking on more responsibilities, and that's mostly because we get overwhelmed by focusing on the obstacles to the outcome. Instead, treat your passion project like a one-hundred-step *process*, and just focus on taking one small step at a time. It's like a friend of mine said after finishing his first marathon: "I didn't run the marathon in twenty-six miles. I ran it in one mile twenty-six times."

FEAR OF MISSING OUT

When I was writing my book *Bliss More*, I didn't have a s cial life. Nearly every Friday and Saturday night f r six months, I was writing. While everyone else was enjoying "Sunday Fundays," I was holed up somewhere writing. Just before midnight n New Year's Eve, I fell asleep on my daybed writing, with the sound of firecrackers going off in the distance. Sure, I had to overcome a lot of FOMO (fear of missing out) during that time, but instead of wishing I didn't have t write, or giving in to the FOM , I chose to see it as an opportunity to challenge the false notion that my happiness was located elsewhere. In that sense, I found my F MO useful, because I got t consciously choose again and again what my real priorities were and how committed I wanted to be t them.

Something More to Consider: Are you in the middle of a project with a deadline, but you keep getting distracted by the fear of missing out, which is making you stall and procrastinate and not make the task the priority it needs to be? What I have found helpful is getting clear on the bigger priority. Let's say it's to be healthier, or to be more abundant, or to strengthen your family ties: start by writing it down. Tie your daily tasks to your top priority, and when you get distracted, keep reminding yourself of your larger goal.

YOU STILL WON One day not long ago, I was hiking with an old college buddy, and I challenged him to an impromptu race up a grassy hill. ✦ Although I started off ahead, I ultimately lost the race. It was disappointing because I really thought I could beat him and I only lost by a hair. ✦ But as we slowly walked back down the hill, a bit achy from the intense physical exertion, I thought to myself how grateful I was to have the stamina in my forties to even run an impromptu uphill sprint, and to have access to beautiful hikes, and to have a dear friend to race against, and to have a sense of humor that allowed me to meet my defeat with a smile, and so much more. ✦ Ultimately, I realized that I actually won by simply being able to have the experience, and I believe the same is true for us all. Again and again, we experience defeat—but if we look closer, we may be able to see an abundance of blessings as well. And while defeats are inevitable, if we can get into the habit of counting up those blessings, the math will show that we still won.

The New York subway has signs that read, "If you see something, say something"—meaning, if you notice anything shady or anyone who looks suspicious, let the authorities know. ✦ But the opposite is also important: as we go about our day, if we see someone doing good, standing up for others, or just being an amazing human, we should say something to them too. We should go up and acknowledge them, and thank them for their courage, or generosity, or compassion. ✦ Why? Because taking a moment to recognize another person for their random act of kindness encourages us all to keep being kind and doing the right thing—even when we don't think anyone else notices or cares.

Some of my closest friends make fun of me for being so obsessed with college football. So does stand-up comedy. And pugs. But it makes me happy. And things that delight and enthrall us—things that may not have anything to do with money or accomplishments or personal growth. We all have little odd things that delight and enthrall us—things that may not have anything fine without football and comedy. Yes, of course. But it's hardly ever about the surface-level experiences. College football is something I get to bond over and share with my three brothers and father. It's extra special to know that we're all watching the same game and rooting for the same team from different parts of the world. Stand-up reminds me of the humor in life. Two of my former girlfriends had enjoyed while growing up with parents who always made me laugh. It reinforces my admiration for them, always teaching us to find the humor in life. Two of my former girlfriends had pugs, and I guess pugs remind me of what it feels like to be in a loving relationship.

If you don't get why some odd things make your friends, spouse, or children happy, try peeking underneath the hood at the deeper meanings—and with a little more insight and understanding, you may find yourself becoming the protector of their happiness instead of trivializing it.

Something More to Consider: Is there an odd obsession that you have that people have teased you about? Have you explored where the obsession comes from? I find that going through the process of self-discovery with our own obsessions makes it easier to understand and show support for the quirky obsessions of others. It's like having a fun little secret we can share with one another—the hidden reasons why we love the peculiar things we love.

HODOPHOBIA I once met a woman who suffered from hodophobia—the fear of traveling away from home. We didn't get into it at the time because I was busy teaching her how to meditate. But she mentioned it to me about a year later, when she signed up for my retreat to India—which would be her first trip out of the country in twenty-something years. She was nervous, but she didn't let her fear stop her. ✦ Now, most people would look at this and congratulate her for finally facing her fear of traveling. But the trip to India was the side-effect. She faced her fear of traveling by taking her meditation practice seriously a year earlier, as it was her underlying anxiety that was perpetuating the hodophobia—not India or Zika virus or ISIS. Once her anxiety diminished through her daily practice, the irrational fear of traveling was still there, but it no longer held her captive. ✦ Facing a fear doesn't have to be some sort of dramatic confrontation with the symptom. In fact, don't even pay any more attention to the symptom. Just commit to your daily inner work. That way, you can begin chipping away at the root cause of your fears—and you might find yourself waking up one day with the idea to do the very thing you were absolutely petrified to do a year earlier.

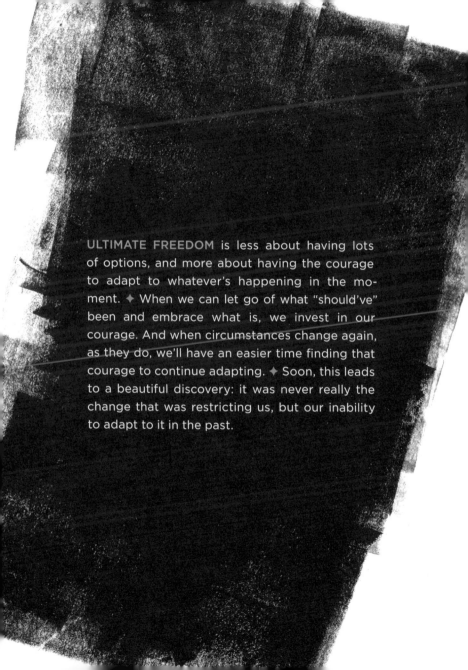

ULTIMATE FREEDOM is less about having lots of options, and more about having the courage to adapt to whatever's happening in the moment. ✦ When we can let go of what "should've" been and embrace what is, we invest in our courage. And when circumstances change again, as they do, we'll have an easier time finding that courage to continue adapting. ✦ Soon, this leads to a beautiful discovery: it was never really the change that was restricting us, but our inability to adapt to it in the past.

USE THE BOOS I read that in 1981, three years before the release of *Purple Rain,* Prince was "chased off stage" during an opening performance for the Rolling Stones in Los Angeles. He was just three songs into his set when dissatisfied audience members began hurling soda cups and hotdog trays at him. This happened in front of ninety-two thousand people. ✦ Now put yourself in Prince's, uh, boots, and imagine the humiliation and embarrassment you would feel if you were following your passion, putting yourself out there, and ninety thousand people started loudly booing and throwing their trash at you, in front of your idols. And Prince is far from the only one. Many other famous musicians have been booed off stage as well, including Lauryn Hill, Kanye West, Drake, Rihanna, and even Beyoncé. ✦ This shows that living in our purpose doesn't make us immune to haters, critics, or even public humiliation— if anything, it's a rite of passage. Like Prince and so many others have done, we must use the boos as fuel for getting better, for continuing to show up, and for believing that no matter how misunderstood we may be now, the tide can always turn and often does, so long as we keep going back on stage.

Something More to Consider: Prince's very public rejection also reminds me of something Andy Warhol once said: "Don't think about making art. Just get it done. Let everyone else decide if it's good or bad—whether they love it or hate it. While they are deciding, make even more art." ✦ The most successful people tend to view rejection as a teacher. From today on, make a practice of writing down five things that you learn from each rejection. And if you can't think of any tangible lessons, then list five ways you can improve the next time.

NO DAYS OFF Bob Marley was shot in his home just two days before he was set to headline a free concert to help unite the political factions in Jamaica. He was warned of more violence if he appeared on stage. ✦ However, he refused to let the threats of violence or his poor health deter him, and he ended up delivering an inspired performance before eighty thousand of his countryfolk —one of the most impactful shows of his career. ✦ When asked why he still played the concert even after being shot and threatened, Marley explained, "The people who are trying to make this world worse aren't taking any days off. So how can I?"

"Is there anything I can do to
make myself enlightened?" the seeker
asked the master. "As little as you can do to
make the sun rise in the morning," the master answered.
"Then of what use are the spiritual exercises you prescribe?"
the seeker replied. "They are to make sure you're not asleep
WHEN THE SUN BEGINS TO SHINE," responded the master.

PHANTOM DELAYS Remember running late one morning to a yoga class I was teaching. ✦ There was bumper-to-bumper traffic at a time and in a place where there was never any traffic. I zigzagged over to the next street, and there was still heavy traffic. I was going to be late, and I hated being late. ✦ After fifteen minutes of inching along in this unexpected traffic jam, it mysteriously cleared up. ✦ I scanned the intersection; there was no sign of anything that could've caused a traffic jam. ✦ When I arrived fifteen minutes late, pissed off about that phantom traffic jam, I saw a maintenance crew sweeping up thousands of shards of broken glass in the front of the room. ✦ Apparently, about ten minutes earlier, when my class was scheduled to begin, a large wall mirror dislodged right behind where I would've been sitting (had I arrived on time) and came crashing down, shattering all over the floor. ✦ I was dumbfounded. That mysterious traffic jam—the one I was cursing all the way to class—was saving my students and me from having a very unlucky start to our day! ✦ Ever since, I've had an improved relationship with unexpected delays. It's not that I get excited about them. I just remind myself that this delay, while inconvenient, could be sparing me from something far worse. So let me just chill out and trust that I'm right where I need to be.

After publishing my first book, *The Inner Gym*, I would check online review sites from time to time to see if any new reviews had posted. I remember gasping when I saw my first one-star review, titled, "LIGHT IS A FRAUD." The reviewer claimed that my book was "new agey garbage" and that I'm a "part of a big money-making scam." I grew angry for a few minutes, and then I became curious to see what the haters had to say about other, more popular self-help titles. Sure enough, the books I cherished the most had all amassed multiple one-star reviews:

"Useless."
*Autobiography
of a Yogi*

"One of the worst
books I've ever read!"
The Power of Now

"Worst novel ever."
The Alchemist

"Mumbo Jumbo."
Be Here Now

It was laughable and equally relieving to see those deeply transformative books also dismissed as complete nonsense by several reviewers—many of whom took the time to outline point by point why the books were so awful. I was reminded of what one of my mentors, writer Steven Pressfield, said about receiving criticism in his excellent book on writing, *The War of Art* (which, coincidentally, was dismissed as "self-help blather" by one reviewer). He said, "It's better to be in the arena, getting stomped by the bull, than to be up in the stands or out in the parking lot."

THE £ONG-TERM €OST

The cost of lying
is our word eventually
becomes worthless.

The cost of being stingy
is people stop being
generous with us.

The cost of being deceitful
is our trust falls into question.

The cost of ignorance
is people don't feel safe
around us.

The cost of gossiping
is people stop
confiding in us.

The cost of being quiet
is people assume
we approve of
their behavior.

I can't remember
doing anything in
life that I've felt
fully prepared to
do before I attempted it—
not writing books, not
teaching meditation class-
es, not running retreats, not asking
someone out on a date, nothing. ✦ The
confidence doesn't usually come until
much later—after trying the thing a few times, and
maybe falling down once or twice. Then you get
some experience under your belt, learn from your
mistakes, and eventually start to feel more prepared. ✦ I know I'm not the only one who's been afraid to
start. And in case you're feeling that way now, I'll share my
little "secret" with you: the final step for getting ready is to
leap into action *before* you feel 100 percent ready. In other
words, stop thinking about it and just go for it. ✦ The most
useful lessons won't happen until after you leap and begin
fumbling your way through the initial stages. And since you
have no idea which mistakes you'll make, you may as well get
on with it so you can start learning from them and building
your confidence in the process . . . BEFORE YOU FEEL READY

PICKING UP THE PIECES Days after I experienced a sudden breakup, I was facilitating a group meditation in my home. One of the meditators—a woman in her late fifties—asked where my girlfriend was, and I told her that we broke up and she moved out. Her eyes began welling up with tears. "What's wrong?" I asked. ✦ "If you can't make a relationship work," she cried, "what hope is there for me?" ✦ "Oh, nooo," I said, "being a meditator or even a meditation teacher doesn't guarantee that our relationships are always going to succeed. But, someone who meditates regularly will usually have an easier time picking up the pieces if and when a relationship comes to an end."

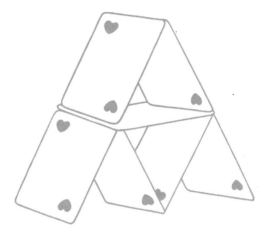

Something More to Consider: We sometimes have extraordinary expectations for ourselves or for others who are committed to their inner work. I've been accused several times of "knowing better" because I'm a meditation teacher, especially in relationships. And I'm quick to remind my partner that even with years of meditation, I may still say or do something that I end up regretting later. In other words, I'm still human. And being a "conscious" human is not about striving for perfection or finding someone who's perfect. It's about being willing to look at your faults and learn from your inevitable mistakes.

```
S  W  E  E  T  Y  I  M  K  E  E  P
B  U  T  T  E  R  F  L  Y  E  T  K
R  F  S  T  A  R  P  O  L  O  U  D
F  M  R  E  S  V  I  F  L  U  C  K
N  L  G  O  D  D  P  C  U  T  E  I
B  I  K  E  G  R  F  L  Y  C  A  N
M  U  S  I  C  T  S  D  A  Y  K  G
Y  P  C  A  R  E  T  M  E  J  O  Y
R  E  A  D  K  I  N  S  P  E  L  L
```

For a long time, I've had this fantasy of each day having its own name. So no more Monday, Tuesday, Wednesday after the first week. The next week would be something like Frogday, Kindday, Moonday, like that. On and on, indefinitely. ✦ I think this would inspire people to not wait until "next Tuesday" to start something they want to do today, because there would only be one Tuesday, and only one Kingday, and one Butterflyday in all of existence. ✦ And what if you wouldn't know what day it was until you woke up? It would be a surprise. Or maybe everyone gets to name their own day? I'm still working out the details. ✦ My point is, let's view each day as special. And treat waking up to each day as a tiny little celebration—a fresh start—because we only have an average of thirty thousand of them in our lives. Use them wisely.

YOU'VE GOT THE WRONG PERSON One of my favorite biblical stories is the one where God calls upon Moses to confront Pharaoh and demand that he release the Israelites from slavery. ✦ Moses's initial reaction was something along the lines of, "Wait, you want me to confront Pharaoh? I think you've got the wrong person for this job." ✦ God replied, "No, you're exactly the person I need for this job." ✦ You see, a lot of us remember Moses as the charismatic leader portrayed by Charlton Heston in the movies. So it's easy to believe that he's fully capable of fulfilling God's directive. ✦ But scholars have revealed the real reason behind Moses's initial hesitation: throughout his entire life, Moses had trouble speaking clearly. Evidently, he was tongue-tied, and some scholars even suggest that he stuttered. ✦ And now God was asking a man with a speech impediment to confront the most powerful (and dangerous) ruler in the land and demand that he free his slaves, or else. Can you imagine? ✦ This story is a metaphor for something we've all grappled with: feeling inadequate to take a leap of faith in the direction of something we're feeling called to do—something that will challenge us to our core, whether it's leaving a job or a spouse, starting over, getting married, or some other massive life change. ✦ We may feel we're not smart enough, skilled enough, connected enough, attractive enough, or wealthy enough for whatever the leap of faith might entail. Or that the consequences of such a bold leap will be too much to bear if it goes south. Moses was no different. And his next question was something we might ask as well if we were in his shoes (or in this case, his sandals): "Alright, supposing I did get in front of Pharaoh, how will I even know what to say?" And God replied, "Just go, and trust that you'll know what to say when the time comes." ✦ The point is to stop over analyzing and take the leap, with full trust that the journey itself will generate all of the resources, the courage, and the knowledge we will need right when we need it. After all, that's why it's called a leap of *faith*.

Something More to Consider: Are you currently in a situation where you're being called upon to take a bold and decisive action, but you feel like you're not ready? We've all been there, and the thing you want to remember is that your readiness is baked into the inspiration to act. Give yourself the benefit of the doubt, and just act as you're called upon to do so, and leave the rest in God's hands.

One Saturday afternoon
when I was young, while walking
home from the library with my
older brother in Montgomery,
Alabama, a police car pulled up
alongside us. I was wearing a
red shirt and my brother was
wearing a green shirt. The officers
got out and told us that there
had been a burglary, and the
suspects were Black boys our age,
our height, and wearing red and
green shirts. ✦ They began questioning
us about where we'd been and where we
were going, which was home. They asked
for our IDs, which we didn't have because we
were too young. And after letting us go, I
remember thinking, wow, what a strange
coincidence that these burglars looked
and dressed exactly like us. ✦ I couldn't
have imagined that the same thing would
happen again a few more times, even into
my adult life. Or that there would be a night
when, in my forties, my girlfriend would
forget to give me a key to her place,
and I would refuse to climb through her
apartment window to take her dogs out
for a walk because I didn't want to be
confused
for a
burglar.

I couldn't have imagined
how many streets I would
cross throughout my adult life to
make white strangers feel safe or
how many people would lock their
doors when I passed their car,
or how many awkward moments
there would be in elevators. In short,
I had no idea that that first stop
with my brother was my
graduation from being seen
as just a boy to being viewed with
suspicion—or that I would normalize
these kinds of incidents so much that
they would be barely worth mentioning to
my white friends, because they just wouldn't
understand. Just like my girlfriend
never understood why I wouldn't climb
through that window. ✦ In life, we may
encounter people or belief systems that
sometimes make us doubt ourselves or
create false assumptions about one another.
And while it's not our fault that these
systems were created, it is our
responsibility to do something
about it. We can start by sharing
our experience with others; or, if
more appropriate, we can seek to
understand
someone
else's.

THE POWER OF SMALL THINGS At various points in my life, I've given up meat, fish, dairy, cooked foods, carbs, alcohol, sugar, and even sex. But so far, the hardest thing I ever gave up was . . . lip balm. I was so addicted to lip balm that I would carry two or three tubes on me at all times, because if I didn't apply it to my lips every five or ten minutes, I would get anxious, my lips would become severely chapped, and I couldn't focus on anything else. ✦ One day, after I accidentally misplaced all three of my tubes of lip balm and had a mini freakout, I decided to quit cold turkey. No longer did I want to be a slave to the lip balm. For the first few days, my lips were drier than cardboard in the sand. Then the cracking started, and I began licking my lips more than LL Cool J eating a popsicle in the summer. Slowly but surely, my lips became less dry, and I remember waking up about a month later and realizing that my lips were naturally moisturized. And they've stayed that way ever since. ✦ Lasting change has always been more of a marathon than a sprint, and it often involves moving through a very trying time in the middle, as the old habit is weakening. Like a mosquito in the bedroom, it's the small things that often wreak the most havoc on larger areas of our life. And it's limiting or managing those small things that can sometimes lead to big improvements in other more important areas (such as our ability to focus). What's something small you can change today that may lead to more freedom in other, larger areas of your life tomorrow?

I remember ordering shirts from a retailer as a teen and being disappointed and confused when the clothes arrived because they always had a boxier fit than they looked like they had on the model in the catalog. ✕ When I became a fashion model many years later, I discovered why the clothes always fit the model so perfectly: on shoots, the stylists would pin, tuck, and clamp the clothing into a flawlessly tailored shape for the camera. Sometimes we couldn't even move without the clothes coming apart. So the whole tailored look was basically an illusion. ✕ Nowadays, whether on social media, dating apps, or YouTube videos, we're being inundated by illusions of perfection. We could even call ours a culture of perfection, because we're all literally "filtered" to some degree. ✕ But if we could peek behind the images, we'd find all kinds of PINS, TUCKS, AND CLAMPS holding them together—which is not a problem as long as (a) we are well aware that most of what we see as "perfect" is an illusion, and (b) we don't compare ourself or our life to someone else's highlight reel of perfection.

Something More to Consider: When I lived in Los Angeles and taught meditation to celebrities, I heard many firsthand reports of the loneliness, unhappiness, debilitating anxiety, and deep-seated insecurities that some of the biggest actors, musicians, and even comedians cope with on a daily basis. Revealing this is simply a reminder that what we see projected onto the screen and what people are experiencing behind the scenes can be, and often is, completely different. As singer Lauryn Hill once admitted to her audience: "There are no big shots in reality, y'all. We're all in the same boat, dealing with the same issues. Same problems. Same stuff."

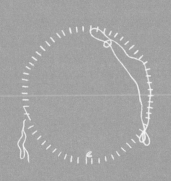

THE RAREST FRIEND Once, I remember sharing some minimalism plans with a couple of friends, and they said in unison, "Okay, now you're going too far!" ✦ That response used to make me doubt myself and second-guess what I was intending to do. Now I see it as confirmation that I'm doing exactly what I'm supposed to be doing, because who wants to live within the confines of other people's comfort-zone-based opinions? ✦ We can't reach our potential if we're unwilling to break free of what's expected of us—even by our closest friends. And because of this, when friends want to try something new and different (in the name of following their inner guidance), we're not helping them by suggesting that they are going too far. After all, we don't know what their deeper spiritual journey entails, so why cage them inside of our fears and expectations? ✦ I say, be the rarest type of friend, who supports others regardless of what you believe is possible for them. Replace empty, knee-jerk warnings and third-generation cautionary tales with patient curiosity. Ask questions. Offer to help them if you can. And maybe they fail—or maybe they succeed. It really doesn't matter, because as far as I can tell, playing it safe doesn't stop people from failing any less. If anything, those who are afraid to try something new or unproven just end up failing with more regrets.

Everything we will do, everyone we will make; every love, every job we will work, every chance we will take, will happen within the span of just 30,000 days. That's how long the average human lives. 30,000 DAYS (80 years), if we're lucky. This fact gives new weight to the following questions: How are we choosing to spend each day? What have we not done that we've always wanted to do? How can we maximize the rest of our time? As the days and nights continue to pass, let us do whatever we can to make the most of each one.

CULTIVATED WITHIN When I had my first real job—the one after college—it was at an ad agency. I worked there for about three months. I loved the work itself. But when I looked at my colleagues who'd been there the longest, from the owner on down, although they seemed like nice people and had many achievements, there was no one who seemed particularly fulfilled. ✦ They all seemed to be searching for something more—the next deal, the next vacation, the next promotion. And here we were, spending eight to ten hours together every day, participating in this collective search for more. ✦ So I quit. I figured, if I'm going to risk being unfulfilled, it's not going to be because of some career path that I was too afraid to leave. ✦ Now, I probably could've made a lot more money in my life had I continued working in advertising. Perhaps I would've won an award or two, and gotten promoted to creative director. But I doubt that would have led to the quality of fulfillment I was ultimately after. ✦ And two decades later, as I write this story from an Airbnb, with hardly any savings, no property, no car, and only a backpack with a couple of days' worth of clothing to my name, I've never felt more fulfilled inside. And I've learned over the years that fulfillment was never about what we accumulate on the outside, but what we cultivate within.

if you can live
without caffeine,

if you can resist
complaining,

if you can ignore a friend's limited
education and never correct him or
her, if you can resist treating a rich
friend better than a poor friend,

if you can be
cheerful, ignoring
aches and pains

if you can take
criticism and blame
without resentment,

if you can understand when
your loved ones are too
busy to give you any time,

if you can
sleep without
the aid of drugs,

IF YOU
CAN

if you can face the
world without lies
and deceit, if you
can conquer tension
without medical help,
if you can relax
without liquor,

if you can honestly
say that deep in your
heart you have no
prejudice against
creed, color, religion,
gender preference,
or politics,

. . . then you have almost
reached the same
level of spiritual
development
as your dog!

When
commissioned to
create a statue of David (from
the biblical story of David and Goliath),
twenty-six-year-old Michelangelo di Lodovico
Buonarroti Simoni didn't go hunting for a block of
marble that resembled David. Instead, he was provided
with a block of "poor quality" marble that other sculptors
had deemed useless. He accepted the challenge and over
two years created what is still heralded as the most masterful
sculpture ever. When asked about his process, he said that he
envisioned what he wanted the statue to look like and began
chipping away at everything that wasn't David. The same goes
for the life we want to create. It doesn't have to be perfect,
so long as we have a clear vision of what we want it to look
like (by identifying our value system for love, for friend-
ship, for work, finances, service, spirituality, etc.).
Then we begin the process of carefully
chipping away at everything that
doesn't align with those
values.

Something More to Consider: Before thinking about specific experiences that you'd like to have in life, it may be helpful to contemplate your values. What are your top five values if you had to name them quickly? In other words, what's important to you from a moral standpoint? Once you articulate your values and get clear about them, you'll be in a better position to edit out anything that doesn't align with them. And your ideal life will begin to naturally emerge by acting from your stated values, in the same way that Michelangelo's famous David emerged from that poor-quality marble.

FLIPPING THE FRUSTRATION Once, on a flight from Los Angeles to New York, I brought my own meal, snacks, and water. The flight attendants repeatedly offered all the passengers beverages and snacks and volunteered to take our trash. ✦ I noticed myself growing irritable because I felt like the flight attendants kept interrupting me to ask if I needed anything while it was obvious (to me) that I had everything I needed. ✦ So around the fourth time an attendant offered me water, I felt myself becoming reactive. But somehow, I was able to flip it, and I found myself saying, "I don't need the water . . . but I just want to acknowledge the incredible service that you and your colleagues are providing for us passengers." ✦ Talking about myself, I continued, "It must be hard getting ignored by some of the passengers while just doing your job. And you all are really going the extra mile to make us feel so cared for, and so special, and I'm just grateful to be the beneficiary of all of the effort you're putting into your work. So I just wanted to say *thank you*." ✦ Man, you've never seen someone more appreciative than that flight attendant. As she lit up, I started to feel connected and present to the moment in a way that I wasn't before. It literally shifted my entire vibe during the rest of the flight. ✦ The flight attendant thanked me profusely, and a conversation that lasted not even five minutes kept me "high" the rest of the flight—and long after I left the airport. ✦ It was a great reminder of the lasting effects of gratitude, and to always look for sincere ways to flip frustration into appreciation.

FLIPPING THE FRUSTRATION Once, on a flight from Los Angeles to New York, I brought my own meal, snacks, and water. The flight attendants repeatedly offered all the passengers beverages and snacks and volunteered to take our trash. ✦ I noticed myself growing irritable because I felt like the flight attendants kept interrupting me to ask if I needed anything while it was obvious (to me) that I had everything I needed. ✦ So around the fourth time an attendant offered me water, I felt myself becoming reactive. But somehow, I was able to flip it, and I found myself saying, "I don't need the water . . . but I just want to acknowledge the incredible service that you and your colleagues are providing for us passengers." ✦ Talking about myself, I continued, "It must be hard getting ignored by some of the passengers while just doing your job. And you all are really going the extra mile to make us feel so cared for, and so special, and I'm just grateful to be the beneficiary of all of the effort you're putting into your work. So I just wanted to say thank you." ✦ Man, you've never seen someone more appreciative than that flight attendant. As she lit up, I started to feel connected and present to the moment in a way that I wasn't before. It literally shifted my entire vibe during the rest of the flight. ✦ The flight attendant thanked me profusely, and a conversation that lasted not even five minutes kept me "high" the rest of the flight—and long after I left the airport. ✦ It was a great reminder of the lasting effects of gratitude, and to always look for sincere

Coming out of meditation, a wise woman noticed a precious stone protruding from the ground next to where she was sitting along the bank of a stream. She carefully dug it out, brushed away the soil, and placed the beautiful jewel in her bag. ✦ The next day, a hungry traveler approached and asked the woman for something to eat. As she reached into her bag for a piece of bread, he saw the shiny stone and, knowing its value, he imagined how owning it could provide him with a lifetime of financial security. ✦ So he asked for the stone instead. Without hesitation, the woman handed it to him, along with some bread. He then left, ecstatic over his good fortune and the knowledge that he was now secure. ✦ A few days later the traveler returned, handing the woman back her stone. "I've been thinking," he said. "Although I know how valuable this stone is, I'm returning it to you in the hopes that you could give me something even more valuable." ✦ "What would that be?" the wise woman asked. ✦ "Could you please teach me about what you have inside of you that allowed you to give me the stone?"

Something More to Consider: This story reminds me of something that I've heard my mentor Rev. Michael Beckwith say several times in talks and interviews: "Don't listen to what I'm saying. *Listen to what I'm listening to.*" The closer we can get to the source, the more aligned our actions and motives become. This is why our highest path is not about accumulating more. Rather, it's about swapping out that which we thought we needed to be happy in exchange for access to the source of happiness within.

My MOM, bless her
heart, loves to tell me
how to drive. "Go!" "Slow down!"
"Hurry up and make this light." "Turn
here!" "Be careful." "Stop!" It used to get under
my skin. For years, when I would come home to visit,
the simple act of driving with my mom seemed to
undo years of meditation. ✦ It's gotten much easier
to cope with now. Because I realize that a day is coming when I'll miss having her around to micro-manage
my driving. So I remember to be appreciative that she's
still here, and that I can still come home to spend
precious time with her. And that she's healthy, and
that she cares enough about me to tell me
how to drive. ✦ It can still be annoying
sometimes, but there's so much
more to be grateful for.

Something More to Consider: Do you have a parent, a sibling, or a spouse who annoys you? And can you easily make a list of ten or twenty things about that person that get under your skin? What about the things you like about them? There's a day coming when they will no longer be around. When that day arrives, what are some of the things that you imagine you would miss about them? If you can remember to think about the things you're going to miss when they're no longer around, it may make the moments when they annoy you much more tolerable.

One evening before bed, a man prayed to understand the real meaning of Heaven and Hell. In his dream that night, he was shown two doors. Inside the first one, he saw people sitting around a huge round table with a large pot of delicious-smelling stew in the center. The man's mouth began to water, until he noticed something odd: the misery and groans of the people sitting around the table. They were thin, sickly, and starving. This must be Hell, he surmised. But how could they be starving with so much food? Then he noticed why. They were each holding onto spoons with handles that were longer than their own arms, making it impossible for them to feed themselves, no matter how hard they tried. What a cruel way to suffer, he thought, leaving the room immediately.

Behind the second door, the setting appeared identical. There was the massive round table with the large pot of the same wonderful-smelling stew, and the people had similar long-handled spoons—except in this room they all appeared cheerful, inviting, and well nourished. Slowly, the man noticed the difference: the people in the second room were using their long spoons to feed one another. And he understood what Heaven truly means: it's not about the quality of the place or the number of resources. The spirit of Heaven is created whenever we share what we have with one another.

TURN A LIFE AROUND I was once leading a meditation teacher training at an ashram in northern India. It was just myself, the five trainees, and the ashram chef, who handled everything from cooking to organizing our laundry pickups to arranging for the cleaning of the rooms. ✦ He was a sweet man—tall, thin, boyish looking. His wife and kids lived too far away for him to travel home each night, so he would stay somewhere on the property, and when he wasn't cooking his heart out for us three times a day, you could sometimes see him taking power naps on the flat roof, or speaking with his wife on the phone, or hanging with the locals. ✦ He occasionally tried to communicate with us to see which foods we liked, but he didn't speak much English and none of us spoke Hindi. So we did that charades thing you do with people who don't speak your language. We speculated from his mannerisms that he was a very funny person in his native tongue. But you can't properly know someone's humor without speaking their language. ✦ Anyway, we decided to acknowledge our chef's dedication to providing us with wonderfully tasty meals by giving him the universal sign of praise—an impromptu ovation. So one day, when he came in to collect our lunch trays, on the count of three, we all broke out into continuous applause. ✦ At first, he appeared shocked, and then he smiled from ear to ear, and then he shyly backed his way into the kitchen. It was a wonderful little moment. Didn't cost us anything to do it. And I imagine it was something he proudly mentioned to his wife and friends when he spoke to them later that day. Maybe he'll remember that moment for the rest of his life. ✦ It reminds me of a quote by Leo Buscaglia: "Too often we underestimate the power of a touch, a smile, a kind word, a listening ear, an honest compliment, or the smallest act of caring, all of which have the potential to turn a life around." ✦ If you see an opportunity today to offer a small gesture of appreciation or sign of gratitude to someone who crosses your path, I encourage you to go for it. Who knows; your kind gesture may brighten up someone's day in the most unexpected way.

THE LAST DAY I came across a thread on Reddit in which people who had planned to attempt suicide anonymously described their "last day." Here's one last-day post that I found particularly moving: "I woke up, watched *Buffy*, ate pizza, called my brother, went to work, came home, and watched the end of the series of *Buffy*. ✦ It may sound like a joke, but I got up after finishing *Buffy the Vampire Slayer* and went walking. I kept listening to 'Gangster's [sic] Paradise' on my iPod until I reached the Aurora Bridge (I live in Seattle). If you know the bridge, you may know that in the last couple years they have built very high fences around it, but when I was there, there was just a small handrail. ✦ I walked to the middle of the bridge and looked down for a while. This part of the bridge was over land and not water, so I continued to walk until I wasn't above someone's yard. I was probably 100 yards before the end of the bridge. I stood looking over the railing for 10 minutes, maybe more. ✦ A man got off the 16 bus at the stop right before the bridge and walked toward me. He stopped beside me and asked if I was okay, and I didn't reply for a while. He just stood next to me for a while and just kept talking. He never stopped talking. He talked about the bridge and the bus and his family and about his work, and chatted away for a solid ten minutes. ✦ He asked where I lived and I told him. He put his hand on my back and coerced me off the bridge and onto a bus. He bussed me home and walked me to my front door. I never got his name, and I haven't seen him since, but he saved my life. ✦ I don't know that I would ever have killed myself, but that's the closest I ever came to it. A stranger saved me and I really hope he knows that."

BIG PROBLEMS There was once a guru who had a knack for helping people solve their biggest problems in a unique way. ✦ As the famous problem-solving guru visited one particular township, he summoned all of the people with problems to assemble together in the town center. The turnout was massive, as everybody came with the hope of having the guru liberate them from their biggest problem. ✦ The guru explained that because of karmic reasons he could not make a problem completely disappear, but he was capable of facilitating the transference of the problem to someone else with a less severe problem. ✦ Next, he instructed his aides to pass around slips of paper to all of those gathered, and he told each person to write down their biggest problem on an individual slip of paper and drop it into one of several buckets that were provided. ✦ After the last person dropped their problem into the bucket, the guru began passing the buckets around and told everyone to sift through the slips of paper to find another problem that they could live with. ✦ "When you find a problem not as bad as yours," the guru instructed, "bring it to me, and using alchemy, I will transfer that new problem to you, while giving your old problem away to another." ✦ The people rummaged through the buckets, analyzing problem after problem, to see which one would be a better problem than their original problem. By the end, everyone had taken back their own problem, only now they felt relieved about it, knowing that their problems weren't nearly as horrific as everyone else's.

WHAT FLOWS OUT My most creative times are not when I'm writing, painting, or doodling. It's when I'm meditating. That's when the dots tend to connect, the hunches form, and the impulses brew. ✦ My writing and other creative expressions are merely the by-products of what gets incubated while I'm sitting with my eyes closed. Then I'll return to the page and start transcribing what I hear. And that becomes the basis of most of these stories and transmissions. ✦ If I wasn't making the time to sit still each morning, usually before I write, I highly doubt that I would be able to keep generating new things to write about—at least not without going completely mad. ✦ If you are in a creative slump, try this: sit with your back supported and eyes closed, and just let your mind roam, swirl, and settle for a good fifteen to twenty minutes. Don't focus on anything in particular. Don't meditate on anything. Just be with your thoughts, whatever they are. Then, go back to the page or the canvas, and see what flows out.

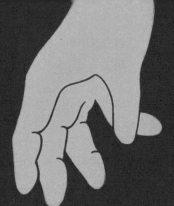

In India, they have a clever way of CATCHING MONKEYS.

Monkey catchers bore a small hole into a coconut and pour out the coconut milk, then stuff peanuts and other little treats inside. Next, they bury it in the ground, deep enough that it can't be easily pulled out, with the small hole remaining exposed. As the monkeys come along, they detect the aroma inside the hole and squeeze their hand into the coconut to grab some treats. Because the hole is big enough to wiggle their hand inside but not big enough to pull out a fist full of treats, they essentially trap themselves. For some reason, it never occurs to the monkeys to just let go of the treats in order to free their hand, and as a result, they are easily caught. The lesson: sometimes it's not holding on tighter that will lead to the happiness we seek; it's letting go.

Something More to Consider: while no one can say what would make you happy, if something feels like a struggle to hold onto because you think it's the source of your happiness, it may be worthwhile to see what would happen if you let go of it. What you will most likely discover is that you are going to be fine without it, and that letting go—while difficult—was the key to your liberation. But doing this requires practice. So start now with letting go of little things, small preferences, and it'll be easier to let go of the bigger things that cause more pain than it's worth holding onto.

FISH LOVE

I once saw a video on social media with a poignant message about love. Here's a loose transcription:

A wise man sees a young man eating fish and asks, "Why are you eating that fish?" The young man responds, "Because I love fish."

"Oh, you love the fish? Don't tell me you love the fish," said the wise man. "What you mean is you love *yourself*. And because the fish tastes good to you, you took it out of the water, killed it, and boiled it." Most of us who talk about love are really talking about "fish love." If a young couple falls in love, it usually means the man sees in the woman someone who he feels can provide him with all of his physical and emotional needs. And she feels that he can provide her with all of her needs. That is usually what we mean by "love"—each person looking out for their own needs. But it's rarely about love for the other. The other person becomes a vehicle for our gratification. It's all *fish* love.

External love is not about what I'm going to get, but what can I give? People make a mistake in thinking that you give to those whom you love, but the reality is you love those to whom you give. True love is a love of giving, not a love of receiving.

WHAT'S POSSIBLE A man was passing by some adult elephants and noticed that they were each being held by the tiniest rope tied to their front leg. ✦ It was obvious that they could break away at any time, but for some reason they didn't. He asked the trainer why these massive animals made no attempt to escape. ✦ When they are young, the trainer explained, we use the same size rope to keep them in place. And as they grow to full size, they become conditioned to believe that the rope is more powerful than it actually is, so they never even try to break free. ✦ Are there any tiny beliefs keeping you from accessing your massive potential? A good place to start is by examining your old, unchallenged assumptions about what's possible for other people, but not for you.

LIFE IS GOOD One of my darkest days was back when I lived in Harlem. My long-term relationship was ending, and I remember being holed up alone in my apartment listening to the Stevie Wonder anthology over and over. ✦ By that point, I'd read a lot of self-help books, and even had a regular yoga and meditation practice. But for some reason, nothing was able to penetrate my spirit like Stevie singing "Don't You Worry 'Bout a Thing." ✦ Although I love the silence, the right song can invoke its own spiritual experience. Which songs get you through the dark times? Maybe create a playlist called "Life Is Good," for those days when you forget just how amazing you are.

YOUR BRILLIANT IDEA Sometimes I'll wake up with what I think is an amazing idea for one of these daily doses, and yet, when I sit to write it out, the words just don't match my initial feeling. But the simple act of writing a draft or two will often lead to a new idea, and drafting the new idea will lead to an even better idea—and more often than not, it's the third or fourth idea that I'll end up going with. ✦ Life is similar. Our first attempt at executing an amazing idea will probably not lead to the amazing outcome of our imagination. But it may teach us something that will lead to another innovation or opportunity that we weren't even thinking about and couldn't have imagined had we not attempted the first or second idea. ✦ This is why I tell people who are waiting for the perfect idea to just start with any idea that feels good enough to take action on, because the creative process will happen more quickly through execution than from sitting around debating the merits of each idea. And while your brilliant idea is definitely in there, it probably won't occur to you until after you've already tried to implement three or four other ideas first.

Before
his flight, Jake went
to the airport café, where he
bought a latte and a bag of mini-doughnuts.
He sat at a nearby table with another guy
sitting on the opposite side reading his paper.
After a few moments, Jake opened
the bag of doughnuts and
took one out. ✦ The other
guy looked at Jake, then
reached down and took
out a doughnut as well,
much to Jake's astonish-
ment. ✦ Jake didn't say
anything. It was just one dough-
nut, after all. But a moment later, the guy
took out another mini-doughnut, and
Jake found himself becoming increasingly
annoyed. How dare this rude guy
just take my doughnuts
without asking!

o
o o
o

p
o

s

Jake ate
another doughnut,
leaving only one left. The
newspaper guy reached for the
last doughnut, but before eating
it, he split it in half and offered the
other half to Jake. Then he got up
to catch his flight. ✦ What
a presumptuous jerk,
thought Jake. Except
when Jake got up for
his flight, he saw that
his own bag of dough-
nuts was sitting on top of his
suitcase, untouched. Oops, *he* was the
one who was being an insensitive doughnut
thief! ✦ This is a good reminder to
always give others the benefit of the
doubt, even when we are 100
percent convinced that
we're right.

o

O
ρ
o
s
e
\

MODERN ART

One of the last times I visited a modern art museum, I saw this long piece of styrofoam wrapped in masking tape lying in a corner. At first, it looked like something left behind. Upon closer inspection, I realized it was supposed to be art. And I remember thinking to myself, "Well, hell, I could've done that." I was a bit perturbed that it was even considered good enough to be on display in such a reputable museum. But what's interesting is, to this day, I don't remember much of anything else I saw in that famous art museum except that ugly styrofoam thing. Out of all the art I walked by that day, the piece that I initially considered to be discarded trash has lingered with me—not because of its hidden beauty or anything like that, but because it dared me to have an opinion about it, and perhaps to make art of my own. And maybe that's the (unintended) goal of an artist—to smoke us spectators out of our little opinionated comfort zones and dare us to create something better.

HURT PEOPLE We've all heard the truism, "hurt people hurt people." This cycle will continue until someone—perhaps you—are brave enough to break the chain and resist the temptation to react with more anger. Try compassion, patience, forgiveness. Sure, they will feel less satisfying in the heat of the moment, but they age better with time. HURT PEOPLE

MY
FEETS IS TIRED

During a strategy meeting for the Montgomery bus boycott, Dr. Martin Luther King Jr. said to one of the elderly ladies in attendance, "Now listen, you've been with us from the beginning. So now you go on and start back to ridin' the bus, 'cause you are too old to keep walking." To which the woman replied, "Oh, no. Oh, no. I'm gonna walk just as long as everyone else walks. I'm gonna walk 'til it's over." ✦ Dr. King inquired, "But, aren't your feet tired?" ✦ She said, "Yes, my feets is tired. But my soul is rested."

Something More to Consider: A wise man once said, "A principle isn't a principle until it costs you something." That something is not always money. It could be comfort, convenience, or access. But while the cost is high, the value of living a principled life is worth far more than anything money can buy.

YOUR INTENTIONS WERE GOOD, BUT...

I once saw a healer who gave me some homework practices to do on my own. And I apparently misunderstood his instructions, because when I came back and enthusiastically reported what I had been practicing, he said, "You know, *your intentions were good*, but that wasn't the correct way to do the exercise." ✦ And I thought, what a great way to tell someone they screwed up: "Your intentions were good, but . . ." Because it's true: although we all screw up from time to time, our intentions are generally good—and he started by recognizing that, instead of condemning me for doing it the wrong way. ✦ His acknowledgment more than softened the blow; it kept me engaged and allowed me to remain open and present to the correction, instead of getting defensive and resentful from the condemnation. ✦ Before correcting someone today, start by acknowledging their good intentions, and notice how much more available they are to the correction.

BAD HABITS I was addicted to sugar as a kid—so much so that I would sprinkle sugar on my Frosted Flakes cereal because it wasn't sweet enough for my palate. ✦ In my twenties, I tried to stop eating so much sugar, but I kept asking myself sloppy questions like, "Is eating this one little cookie going to kill me?" ✦ Obviously, the answer is no. Eventually, I learned that I needed to ask myself stronger questions like, "Is eating this one cookie going to help me break my addiction to sugar?" Same answer, different results. ✦ My takeaways from that experiment were simple: 1) It's easy to justify sloppy behavior by asking sloppy questions. 2) Asking sloppy questions is a bad habit just like eating sugar. 3) We can't be sloppy six days of the week and expect to somehow be strong on the seventh. 4) Asking stronger questions is a habit worthy of strengthening.

Something More to Consider: Have you been struggling with addictive behavior? What questions are you asking yourself about it? What's your internal dialogue like? Are you being honest with yourself about the quality of questions you're asking before giving into the addiction? What about with other behaviors? Where do you have discipline? What actions can you export from the strong behavior to the weak behavior?

"A cynic
is a man who
knows the price
of everything
and the value
of nothing."

THE VALUE OF NOTHING Oscar Wilde said, "A cynic is a man who knows the price of everything and the value of nothing." ✦ Once I identified my destiny to become a meditation teacher, I began taking active steps in that direction. I didn't know how it was going to happen. So I did what I could. I shadowed my teacher around for a number of years. Finally, the opportunity to become a teacher presented itself in an intensive three-month training where I would have to drop everything to study in India and northern Arizona. ✦ The problem was the upfront cost of the training: $13,000. At the time, I was making $800 to $900 a week (before taxes) teaching yoga, and I had little to no savings. But I believed in my heart that I was supposed to train to become a meditation teacher with that particular master teacher, so I filled out the application, got accepted, and began preparing to leave for the training. ✦ Meanwhile, time was ticking down for me to pay my tuition. I didn't worry or panic, because I trusted that something was going to happen that would produce the money I needed. And about two days before my tuition was due, I received a random credit card cash advance offer in the mail for $14,000, free of interest for twelve months. ✦ Normally, I didn't pay attention to those kinds of offers, much less consider accepting them, due to the exorbitant interest charged after the initial twelve-month period. But this time was different. I felt it was a godsend and didn't even think twice about using it to pay my tuition. ✦ I went away for the three months, learned what I had to learn, and fifteen years, thousands of lives touched, and a few published books later, I fulfilled my destiny and became a full-time meditation teacher. It was the best thing I ever said yes to in my life. ✦ I share this story because using that credit card advance money to pay for my teacher training would've been red-flagged by many of the financial-freedom gurus of the world as unnecessarily risky, if not completely irresponsible. That's because we have been taught to view money as the source of opportunities—save more money now and have more financial freedom down the line. ✦ But what if it's actually the opposite? What if opportunities of the heart are the source of money, support, and other resources? What if saying yes to what's in our heart generates the necessary resources? And what if rejecting those opportunities due to a scarcity mentality actually drains our resources because, in a way, we rejected our divine inheritance? ✦ It's not for me to say conclusively which is which. But over the years, I've seen a lot of people reject meditation and other activities that they knew would be beneficial for them because they felt like they couldn't afford it. And what I've seen from both sides of the equation is how saying yes to these heartfelt opportunities, even without knowing how they are going to happen financially, never puts us in a worse position—only a better one. ✦ All these years later, I could be writing about how much money I saved back then, and how I was *almost* gullible enough to take that predatory loan to learn how to teach meditation, and how I'm glad that I didn't do it because I know a lot of people who got burned doing that same kind of thing. And I would've been right. ✦ But instead, I'm teaching people how to find happiness within, producing inspirational variety shows, and writing books about inspiration—because I said yes to what was in my heart back in 2007, and even before then. And what ended up happening instead was a lot more exciting and personally inspiring than a story about saving money. ✦ So here's my financial advice: say yes to what's in your heart. Don't worry about how everything's going to unfold. Just work hard and keep taking the next step in the direction of what makes your heart sing.

Epilogue

One of the biggest obstacles to exploring inspiration is the lack of a good reason—meaning, a reason that sounds rational enough to endure the interrogation of our spouse, our peers, our family members, critics, and strangers.

It's been beat into us that we need a good reason to do anything outside of our normal routine.

I remember walking through Union Square in Manhattan late one evening, and the following idea came to me: go into Barnes & Noble and buy a Rubik's Cube, and learn how to solve it. So that's exactly what I did.

I walked into Barnes & Noble about fifteen minutes before the store closed for the night, and bought its last Rubik's Cube.

I didn't have a good reason for doing so, other than the fact that that's what my inner guidance instructed me to do. I also didn't have a lot of free time for playing with a Rubik's Cube budgeted into my schedule. But I went online and found a guide for solving the cube.

When I mentioned to friends what I was doing, the big question was "Why?" And I didn't have a good answer. I honestly didn't know why. But I persisted in learning the algorithm to solve it, which took about a week to master.

And during the learning process, I began to notice something interesting: the way you solve a Rubik's Cube is eerily similar to the way meditation helps to restore balance in the body.

Later, I made a video comparing the two methods and posted it on YouTube. It's called "How Meditation Works Using a Rubik's Cube," if you want to look it up.

It became my first viral video, and it helped thousands of people understand how meditation works by comparing it to something everyone is familiar with.

As a result of that video, I taught an influx of new meditation students.

There's no way I could've imagined that the nudge to purchase a Rubik's Cube and learn how to solve it was going to lead to more teaching opportunities.

If I had let my rational mind stop me from listening to inspiration, things would've probably been fine, but what listening to it does is it turns up the volume on the voice of inspiration, and before long, you see that inspiration is nudging us all of the time, and mainly in the direction of our creative potential, which is always prompting us to speak and behave in unexpected, unplanned ways.

So that's what these doses are about. It's for you to use them to explore your version of the Rubik's Cube, whatever that is. Maybe it's a spontaneous road trip with no destination in mind, an unexpected phone call to an old friend just to say hi, maybe it's popping into the Museum of Ice Cream while you're on your way to file your taxes. Who knows?

The important thing is to say yes to it and stay curious. If you get a whim or a hunch, don't let anyone talk you out of it because it doesn't make sense (to them).

It doesn't need to make sense to anyone for it to qualify as inspiration. In fact, that's one of the telltale signs that you're being guided by something bigger than you. So follow it enthusiastically, every chance you get. That way, you never have to look for inspiration. Inspiration will find you.

Acknowlegments

While all of the doses in this book were composed in my own words over the last five years, many were inspired by other sources, and I want to give credit where possible.

The Dr. Martin Luther King stories in My Obligation and My Feets is Tired were sourced from *My Soul is Rested*, by Howell Raines, and the documentary, *King in the Wilderness*.

The Chris Rock movie I referenced in "Lose Money" is called *I Think I Love My Wife*.

One Step at a Time, Ten Years, The Triple Filter, It's All God, The Cracked Pot, Everything is an Illusion, What Feels Right, The Power to Heal, This is Good, The Shipwreck, When the Sun Begins to Shine, Precious Stone, Spirit of Heaven, Big Problems, and What's Possible are all classic stories that have been told by yoga and meditation teachers forever. The original authors are unknown to me.

Bold in Action and Catching Monkeys are stories I first heard in Transcendental meditation circles. I am not aware of the authors.

Abundance was based on a personal story that was told to me by my dear friend Sina.

The Wrong Note and Your Attitude are stories I developed after stumbling across YouTube interviews of Herbie Hancock and Miles Davis.

I heard author Steven Pressfield mention the cancer initiative I referenced in Dreams Deferred while listening to one of his many podcast interviews.

Morning Prayer, If You Can, Fish Love, and Oops are inspirational pieces I found floating around the net. The originators are unknown to me.

And Last Day was directly copied from a Reddit thread about people who were thinking of committing suicide. The author was understandably anonymous.

Now for the creation of the book:

I want to thank my editor Diana Ventimiglia for believing in this project from day one. Your dedication throughout the process has been palpable. You're the best editor an author can have, and I still can't believe you were inspired to go nomadic after reading the early versions of the manuscript.

I also have eternal gratitude for my illustrator Yuliia Andriichuk and Art Director Lisa Kerans. Thanks for your creativity, and for showing up to our countless brainstorming sessions with fresh ideas and the willingness (and patience) to examine every detail of every design with me. To consider where we started and where we ended up is just mind blowing!

I'd also like to acknowledge my agent Coleen O'Shea for your steady guidance throughout the entire process, and for always making sure that we were hitting our deadlines.

And to the rest of the Sounds True team for being such incredible collaborators. I've never felt so included and supported by a publisher from concept to title to cover to launch.

And a special thanks to Bryndan, Chris, Erin, Ava, Ingrid, and Rosario for your support while writing this book.

Thank you to my family for your love and support. Y'all were my first inspiration in life, and for that I feel extremely blessed.

About the Author

Light Watkins has been a meditation and spiritual teacher for more than 20 years. He is the author of *The Inner Gym* and *Bliss More*, and hosts a weekly podcast about hope called *At the End of the Tunnel*. Light became nomadic in 2018 and now travels the world giving talks on happiness, mindfulness, inspiration, and meditation to sold-out audiences. He's been profiled in *Time, Vogue, Forbes, People,* the *New York Times*, and mindbodygreen. For more, visit lightwatkins.com.

About Sounds True

Sounds True is a multimedia publisher whose mission is to inspire and support personal transformation and spiritual awakening. Founded in 1985 and located in Boulder, Colorado, we work with many of the leading spiritual teachers, thinkers, healers, and visionary artists of our time. We strive with every title to preserve the essential "living wisdom" of the author or artist. It is our goal to create products that not only provide information to a reader or listener but also embody the quality of a wisdom transmission.

For those seeking genuine transformation, Sounds True is your trusted partner. At SoundsTrue.com you will find a wealth of free resources to support your journey, including exclusive weekly audio interviews, free downloads, interactive learning tools, and other special savings on all our titles.

To learn more, please visit SoundsTrue.com/freegifts or call us toll free at 800.333.9185.